Building the New Universities

Building the New Universities

Tony Birks

photographs by **Michael Holford**

Introduction by Peter Cowan
Professor of Planning Studies, University College, London

DAVID & CHARLES
Newton Abbot

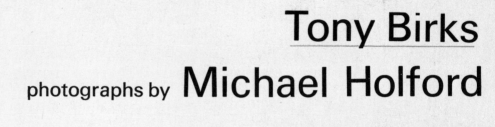

ISBN 0 7153 5476 0

Set in 11 on 12pt Pilgrim
and printed in Great Britain
by Clarke Doble & Brendon Limited
for David & Charles (Publishers) Limited
South Devon House Newton Abbot Devon

The photograph on the title page shows teaching
buildings at the University of East Anglia.

Contents

To the memory of Max Parrish

Introduction

It is a privilege to be given the opportunity to welcome this timely book.

The new universities of the sixties have reached the first point in their development at which their architectural achievement may fairly be appraised. By placing their plans and buildings on record in so penetrating yet sympathetic a manner Tony Birks and Michael Holford have performed a service which amid the preoccupations and excitement of continuing growth might all too easily have been neglected. The critic, the architectural historian and the architect as well as the general reader would have been the poorer for the lack of it and though its main purpose may be to discuss the contribution which the new universities are making to the appearance, so to say, of our times, those concerned with learning and the dissemination of knowledge will also find in it much to reflect upon in the variety of expression which architects are giving to their needs.

Variety is indeed perhaps the sharpest import of this book. All the work shown has been carried out within the programmes of capital allocation authorised by the University Grants Committee who are as concerned with fairness as they are with the obligation to secure good value for the public expenditure for which they accept responsibility. It has all therefore been designed and built within a formula which makes no exceptions.

The results demonstrate vividly that the architects regarded this as a challenge rather than a restriction. Had it been seen only as a constraint we might have expected in response the development and much wider application of a series of standard building types each suitable for one or more of the various kinds of requirements, and each capable of being built from on-site and factory-made components produced in batches; for industrial experience suggests that large scale repetitive operations should result in lower cost for comparable quality.

This is not yet always the case in the building industry which has problems peculiar to itself. Some of the work shown here is of what is known technically as industrialised or 'system' construction. It will be seen however that it contributes to, rather than dominates, the pattern of the whole and, it may be thought, adds to the richness of architectural expression called forth by the challenge of a remarkable decade in the history of higher education.

PETER COWAN

University College
London
December 1971

7

1 A Decade of Expansion

The decade 1960 to 1970 witnessed the greatest expansion in university education in Britain's history. During this decade the number of university students more than doubled from just over 100,000 to 220,000, and the number of universities increased from 22 to 46. Such a startling change, whatever its causes, represents a sustained governmental effort to provide the possibility of university education for all those capable of benefiting from it, in accordance with the Robbins Report of 1963. It has been accompanied by an increased financial dependence by the universities on the State.

In environmental and architectural terms the expansion has provided unprecedented opportunity and made possible a burst of building which has been compared to the great cathedral building movement of the twelfth century. In our own century it can only be compared to the foundation of the new towns. The purpose of this book is to show the impact of the new architecture on the environment and on the lives of the fifty thousand people who are already intimately affected by it. It is important to illustrate the new architecture as fully as possible, and within a small compass it seems sensible to be selective and to assess critically and in some detail seven of the universities which have a common factor in the manner of their foundation, giving particular attention to the concepts of university planning which have grown up in response to the expansion.

Each aspect of university growth, its innovations, its financing, the design of libraries and of student housing, is a special study in itself and the academic structure of the new universities—already widely documented—does not come within the present terms of reference. It is, however, important to trace the recent history of the universities in Britain and the place of the new foundations in the wider context of higher education in general.

Oxford and Cambridge remained until the nineteenth century the only universities in England. The first great revolution of university thinking came in that century with the establishment of London University and the civic foundations in the large population centres. London, an aggregate of institutions founded separately from 1836, has always been a special case, scattered widely across the metropolis, but its physical development shares certain features with the older civic universities such as Manchester, Liverpool, Leeds, and Birmingham. These were founded with local enthusiasm and civic pride, and often with the help of wealthy industrialists. They were non-collegiate and catered chiefly for home-based students, and while London had colleges and a larger proportion of foreign students, both types of university subscribed to teaching by lectures in large lecture halls, and the architecture was

◁ *2. The first students at Britain's new generation of universities entered Falmer House, Sussex, in 1961 through the thirty-six foot high arch in the south façade of this remarkable building designed by Sir Basil Spence.*

structured accordingly. Residential buildings were few and the proliferation of small-scale rooms, so characteristic of Oxford and Cambridge, is absent.

The nineteenth-century academic idiom was monumental, ponderous, and often symmetrical and neo-classic in design. With certain neo-gothic aberrations, the nineteenth-century building in Oxford and Cambridge tended to follow this trend, William Wilkins' campus plan for Downing College, Cambridge (1818) having anticipated the formal, carefully balanced buildings so well exemplified by University College London, a university precinct built in Bloomsbury in 1828. Here, lecture halls, common-rooms and corridors are squeezed into a classical symmetry which takes no account of functional requirements, but which sets an academic style paralleled in some American universities.

The later civic universities such as Reading, Nottingham, Southampton, and Hull each began as a working apprentice to London; each was a university college unable to offer its own degrees and therefore limited in its academic originality. Similarly, the early architecture of these universities was tailored to the academic cut of the parent. All these younger foundations remained small and showed a tiny rate of growth for the first half of this century, with consequently few new buildings. Together with Oxford and Cambridge, the Scottish universities, Durham, the University of Wales and the older Civics, they complete the list of the foundations which existed at the end of World War II.

The University Grants Committee, established in 1919 to administer the allocation of public money to the universities, made cautiously encouraging noises in 1946 in response to a suggestion that a new university college could be founded at Stoke-on-Trent, then one of the most populous areas in Britain without a university. The continuous efforts of Lord Lindsay from Oxford, together with the support of local sponsors, succeeded in establishing a precedent in 1949, when Keele University was formally founded under the auspices of the University Grants Committee. Sponsored by Oxford, Birmingham, and Manchester Universities, it was nevertheless able to issue its own degrees and was not tied to the academic pattern of London University in its degree courses. Keele therefore became the first university founded through the UGC by the State, and financed entirely by State funds. Academically innovatory (with a four-year degree course incorporating a broad foundation year common to all disciplines), it opened the way to the second great revolution in universities—freedom to express new ideas—which was to gather impetus about ten years later. Finally, Keele was the first university consciously to adopt a totally residential formula and a physical setting which later became a standard—an out-of-town campus in spacious grounds. It occupied part of Keele Park, a beautiful area of 4,000 acres.

No sense of urgency inspired the University Grants Committee to establish a minimum growth rate for Lord Lindsay's brainchild, and Keele was intended to increase in numbers slowly and to remain small, although it encouraged a greater equality of numbers between the sexes than was common at the time. In many respects Keele University was the progenitor or forerunner of the new universities of the 1960s, but as the first of the line, it was the one most likely to run blindly into mistakes and failure.

Its failure to appoint from the start a consultant architect to co-ordinate the bricks-and-mortar endeavours in Keele Park resulted in a physical environment so mediocre that it belies the experiment of the university itself. The local

City Architect's Office produced the early faculty, residential, and library buildings in a dreary style characteristic of the municipal architectural standards of the time, hampered by the unavailability of large sums of Treasury money for major schemes. By the time the seven new universities of the 1960s were founded, the appointment of a consultant architect was fortunately regarded as essential.

The great expansion which doubled the number of students and of universities in a single decade has its roots in the mid-1950s, when student numbers stood at about 80,000 and a great increase in applications was anticipated in the early 1960s, as the famous postwar 'bulge' reached the age of 'A' levels. The University Grants Committee's Report of 1953 had stated that 'a marked increase in student numbers will be required from about 1960 onwards if the proportion of each age group which reaches the university is to be maintained', and from 1956 onwards it issued student projections for the mid-1960s, each one revising the previous estimate upwards, and showing an ever sharper rise: 106,000 by the bulge years; then 135,000; then 168,000. It was clear that the existing universities could not cope with such an increase without bursting at the seams, as French universities were to do in the same bulge period.

In 1956, the Director of Education for Brighton, Mr W. G. Stone, put forward a proposal to the University Grants Committee for a university college in Brighton. The plan was backed with much local support, a spacious and elegant site and a promised subvention from the rates to assure financial support as well. Many approaches had been received by the UGC from authorities throughout the country after the successful founding of Keele in 1949, and these had included an earlier approach from Brighton. To the geographical and local advantages of Brighton was now added the increasingly urgent need to take a new step towards solving the problem of student numbers, and the UGC gave its approval to the local promotion board in 1958.

The untried sequence of events which followed became the pattern for later foundations. An Academic Planning Board including prominent members of other universities was proposed, which succeeded the local promotion board in taking over most of the university's affairs. The board prepared a basic academic blueprint and appointed a vice-chancellor. Soon after, other key appointments were made, including that of consultant architect. With the chartering of the university, the Academic Planning Board was dissolved and replaced as a ruling body by the Council of the University.

The momentum generated by the foundation of the University of Sussex in 1958 was increased when the existing universities made it clear that they could not match, unaided, the proposed student figures for the mid-1960s. The UGC in 1959 then set up a Sub-Committee on New Universities, and the government announced its support for six more new foundations.

The initiative remained local. No centralised effort was made to zone universities or to compute relationships between populations and higher educational facilities. The kind of institution which the new universities were going to be was nevertheless forming, and one of the most important early decisions was that the universities were to aim at a figure of 3,000 as the 'minimum viable size'. The Vice-Chancellor of Sussex, Sir John Fulton, had stressed the need for a large and united group of academics to ensure high intellectual standards, and this implied a proportionately large student body. The figure of 3,000 was four times the proposed *ultimate* size for Keele, and only Leeds,

Manchester, Birmingham and Liverpool amongst the civic universities exceeded it in 1959. The new universities were planned to be big by current standards, and what is more, were expected to reach this size within ten years —a revolutionary growth rate with vital implications for architects and planners. They were not necessarily to be founded in large towns, and so the impact on the local community could be expected to be considerable. They were not intended to be regional universities as the earlier Civics had been, with a large local catchment area for students, and so the provision of residence was a high priority. Finally, a special provision made by the Chairman of the University Grants Committee, Sir Keith Murray, was that the new universities should have large sites, with a minimum area of 200 acres. The implications of this condition are discussed in Chapter 2.

The working principle of the UGC was that local proposals would be considered on their merits, with reference to the above conditions, and all other relevant local factors. An area resistant to the idea of having a university planted upon it would therefore not be pressed against its will (local goodwill being a most vital but fugitive factor, especially in the early days). With the increasing mobility of students, geographical plotting of a new map of learning institutions would serve no good purpose. The initiative must come from the regions.

After Brighton, more applications for new universities came pouring in from almost forty areas, many of which, such as Stamford in Lincolnshire, had long cherished the ambition to have their own university. York and Norwich had both made previous appeals to the Crown or the government for universities of their own, and were given UGC approval in 1960. The remaining four universities, Essex, Kent, Warwick, and Lancaster, were approved by the end of the following year, so that the opening of the first of them coincided with the approval of the seventh (Lancaster), in an atmosphere of mounting expansionist pressure anticipated by the establishment of the Robbins Committee to report on the future of higher education.

This famous report, which appeared in 1963, was the first ever to investigate the whole spectrum of higher education in which one half (the technical colleges, etc.) is subject to central control, and the other (the universities) is autonomous. The Robbins Report predicted a massive increase in student numbers to over half a million by 1980, of whom 300,000 would require places in the universities. In order to meet this requirement, expansion and greater equality of status was prescribed for the existing universities. The new universities were to be supplemented by the 'making up' to university level of nine Colleges of Advanced Technology, and at least six further new universities were to be founded, of which one was to be in Scotland.

It was therefore a combination of UGC action taken by 1961 and Robbins' recommendations implemented after 1963 which caused the total number of universities to double, although only one of the six further new foundations (Stirling in Scotland) has since been made. In 1963 the impetus for expansion was at its height and the figures for 1970 showed that the interim targets for student places had been achieved.

The seven UGC foundations and Stirling all had, like Keele, the opportunity to innovate, starting with a clean slate, and all showed in separate ways a reaction to the traditional courses and faculty structures of their predecessors. Thus all instituted greater breadth of courses, many proposing degrees in 'new' subjects. They all showed a reaction against over-specialisation and, above all, invoked flexibility to allow movement from one discipline to another for the individual student who had not yet made up his mind which subject to study in depth. Only Stirling followed the example of Keele, with a broad foundation year as part of the four-year course, and a three-year degree course with many postgraduate opportunities was adopted elsewhere. All of these considerations affected the physical form of the universities, but no decision more so than that a university grand plan, architectural as well as academic, was necessary. The warnings of Dr Geoffrey Templeman, Vice-Chancellor of Kent, that planning in the long term was dangerous and foolish, as the future was uncertain, was an unfashionable comment at the time. It has since been proved justified as financial stringency, public accountability and increasing governmental influence have changed the mood of expansion into one of compression.

The pressure of numbers remained, but by the end of the decade the aim was to inject as many students as possible into existing institutions and into buildings by studying the utilisation of facilities and the application of a system of norms. Greater value for public money in higher education, the maximum number of graduates per million pounds expenditure in the light of the inevitable increase in the total of graduates, had become the guiding principle.

Now that the foundation of further new Robbins universities is no longer contemplated, the opportunity to think afresh and implement new ideas can be seen to have come and gone within ten years, for once an institution is established in its own image, it is difficult to change. Fortunately, a great deal of fresh thinking did take place during the decade, both in academic and in environmental planning, and the more flexible and open-ended plans will survive better as external factors change about them and influence them. A progressive increase in the declared optimum size of the new universities was readily absorbed into the environmental planning—it was even anticipated by some of the consultant architects. As early as 1963, Dr Albert Sloman, Vice-Chancellor of Essex University, announced in his celebrated Reith Lectures long-term plans for a university of 20,000, an American-sized giant which shocked traditionalists, but which exactly matched the flavour of the Robbins Report. Essex was followed by Warwick with an equally ambitious scheme.

That the new universities will expand is certain, but that their facilities will keep pace with increasing numbers is uncertain. In the interests of increased efficiency, some universities may pool their resources, and the next decade may see the emergence of the Polyversity, as the last one showed the flourishing of individuality. Keele University was founded as an isolated experiment in a period of caution; the seven inheritors of the mantle of Keele owe their foundation jointly to the pressure of numbers and a feeling of a need for change. New ideas in university education are said to have weighed equally with the need to provide university places when the UGC approved the foundation of the Seven, and the built-in inferiority complex of the apprenticeship period undergone by the smaller Civics was avoided. By deliberately allowing the new foundations to develop in their separate ways, with only informal contact, the University Grants Committee also managed to avoid too precise a 'formula', albeit new, for the universities which were going to rise in different places around the country. Similarly, no architectural parameters were specified, and the seven new foundations started enthusiastically with what Professor Asa Briggs described as 'psychological élan'.

2 Sites and Plans

Of the seven centres—the Shakespearian Seven, as they are known to the University Grants Committee because of the ring of their names—all had made a previous attempt to get themselves a university, apart from Essex, and here the initiative was taken by the county and the choice of town lay between Chelmsford and Colchester. Before any proposal would be seriously considered by the UGC, it required a guarantee of some measure of local financial support (usually from the rates), an available site of about 200 acres (often also presented by the local authority) and an assurance of lodgings within easy reach. Colchester was preferred to Chelmsford in Essex partly because it was twenty miles farther from the magnetic pull of London. Even so it was, with two of the other selected centres, Brighton and Canterbury, within an hour's train journey of London, a fact which encourages students to go off for weekends and academic staff to commute from the capital. Such influences fragment the social side of a university and work against the concept of a 'total community'.

The problem of student residence appeared to be neatly simplified for Sussex when the University was founded in Brighton, for the term-time demand for accommodation coincided exactly with the off-season slack in local hotels and boarding-houses. When York and East Anglia Universities were given approval, their promotion boards had organised lodgings locally for 500 students in each of the cities concerned. But lodgings are limited in towns which do not have a holiday trade, and they do not get more numerous with an increase in demand. Among the local authorities trying to promote universities those such as Bournemouth and Blackpool, with ready-made accommodation, had a distinct advantage, and when approval was given for Essex at Colchester, near Brightlingsea and Clacton, and Kent at Canterbury, near Herne Bay and Whitstable, these seaside towns were seen as a safety valve. Lancaster, in due course, was even more dependent on Morecambe, and when Coventry was chosen for the University of Warwick, nearby Leamington Spa could furnish a limited amount of similar accommodation.

The chosen towns vary in size by a factor of ten from 33,000 at Canterbury, with no large towns nearby, to 335,000 at Coventry in the heart of the populous Midlands, and so an average figure is meaningless. York, however, with a local population of something over 100,000 and a university-orientated population of something over 7,000 (students, academic staff, administration, general staff and families) perhaps represents a healthy numerical proportion of 7 per cent, by which the university can make a major cultural impact on the community without being the be-all and end-all of the town, and without

◁ *3. A skyline of arresting shapes at Lancaster University. The last of the Seven to be designed, Lancaster has the most concentrated plan, with buildings clustering about a linear axis like nails around a bar magnet. The axis is a pedestrian routeway or spine which runs diagonally across the picture.*

15

inspiring hostility from townsmen because of its encroachment on their standard way of life.

Much more important than the size ratio, however, is the actual physical relationship between the university and the town. Sir Keith Murray's insistence on a site of about 200 acres, so that the university should not be cut off from its sports facilities, is the principal reason for the out-of-town location of all of the Seven. The decline in sports participation by undergraduates since 1960 may be reversed at a later stage, but the implication of a campus surrounded by football pitches and green fields, and cut off from its town, makes the issue the most hotly debated by critics of the foundations. If 200 unrestricted acres had been available within a suitable town, the UGC would have been delighted, but apart from the high cost of urban acres, the Committee was circumscribed in making the best possible choice of site by all sorts of factors, from commercial interests to Roman remains. Decisions of expediency based on the condition of size result in all Seven being in roughly the same sort of place—universities in a park or parkland area, well beyond walking distance of the town. Like the Victorian public boarding-schools founded in the nineteenth century, the campuses are not contaminated by the unclean air of the cities, but on average the majority of the students nevertheless lodge in the city, and have their lives split like any commuter. 'Going to the university', a phrase which in a different context disappeared from the vernacular between the wars, reappears in a local context associated with windy bus stops and long waits.

The aspiration for a latterday Oxford or Cambridge, with the university units intertwined with commercial and other elements in the town is a most appealing one, though difficult to organise. It could be brought about in two ways. Firstly, a new-town site could be chosen and a university planned in its midst so that the two could grow together in the same symbiotic relationship as in Oxford in medieval times. When new towns were originally being planned to provide housing for young families, universities were not thought of. Only when the young families grew near the age for GCE exams did the pressure move to university expansion, and naturally many of the students of today go home to new towns in the vacation. Since new towns often have social problems because of the lack of a 'heart', it is a great pity that at Stevenage, for example, the opportunity to provide this heart, by building a university, was missed. The Open University is doing just this by siting itself at Milton Keynes, where it will provide a cultural nucleus for the new city, though of course the Open University, educating students by 'remote control', involves far fewer people in the immediate area.

A second method of bringing the heart of a new university and town together is to make use of available spaces in existing towns which have reached the stage of growth or age so familiar in American cities, where the centre has become neglected and the immediate periphery is the most active region.

Catching a town in the process of urban renewal and building a university in the central spaces almost certainly means a fragmentation of the university site, but there are many who regard this as an insignificant disadvantage. On this basis, there might have been a University of Worcester (instead of a University of Warwick) in the reorganised area around the cathedral, or a University of Chester, where the traditional principle of segregating pedestrians and vehicles by elevated walkways could easily have been continued into the university.

Of the centres chosen, all except Warwick are related to ancient towns with old cathedral or cultural backgrounds, and even the Midlands' new university only has to look ten miles to its putative parent, the town of Warwick. Those who criticise the choice of elderly towns as hosts instead of the fast-growing industrial towns like Swindon and Basingstoke are confounded by the preference of many of the students themselves. Application figures suggest that amongst provincial choices, those which can offer local amenities and a promise of some cloistered quiet are as attractive to potential students from all backgrounds as trendy cities.

In the context of innovation, it is unadventurous to say the least that seven roughly contemporary universities should have set off with identical target figures and similar sites, although both represented an expression of the optima of the time. Perhaps at least one of the universities should have been planned from the start to be much larger than the others, to accommodate large-scale research teams, as argued by John Maddox, addressing the Sussex seminar on university planning. Certainly, at least one of them should have been inside a town.

Lionel Brett, writing in the *Architectural Review* of October 1963, declared:

> Any activity (with the exception no doubt of pure contemplation) that takes itself out of the city or refuses to come into it impoverishes the city and impoverishes itself. For the city it is the loss of youth in its streets and pubs and coffee bars, the loss of a bit of help in shouldering the burden of urban renewal, the loss of a bit of variety and vitality in the townscape. For the university it is the subtle threat of a new kind of public school segregation amongst goal posts.

By the time he had written, it was far too late. A public enquiry in Norwich in 1961 had shown the size of local opposition to a central site and the new foundations were all in too much of a hurry to pick their way through local problems. Opportunities of large sites outside the towns were seized by the promotion boards *before* approval came from the UGC, as part of the necessary procedure, so the urban university never got a chance.

At Lancaster and Norwich opportunities did occur to develop sites within the cities. At Lancaster, the area around the castle was due for renewal, and at Norwich an actual site of thirty acres around Ber Street was offered, sloping down to the River Yare, and near to the railway station. If this had been used as the main site, further developments could have taken place in several of the numerous city church precincts which had become decrepit. These smaller sites would have been appropriately developed as residential areas housing students in compact communities if not in colleges, and a latterday Oxford *might* have emerged. The Norwich Public Enquiry in 1961, which did its best to promote this view, was really held, however, because of the opposition to the alternative site, a municipal golf course adjacent to the city's Earlham Park, and an ideal landscape environment. The golfers lost the day and their golf course. In any event, the UGC required more acreage than the Ber Street site provided. This site has since been covered with municipal housing and has revealed geological problems which would have plagued the university, but not, I believe, defeated it. The principle, nevertheless, remains the same.

In every instance except York, the local authorities—city or county or a combination of the two—shared the cost of the site, and gave it as a free present to the university. And York received help from the Rowntree Trust. In four cases the land represented a park, with a country house attached. Wivenhoe Park at Colchester and Heslington Hall at York were bought from the resident owners, and Stanmer Park and Earlham Park at Brighton and Norwich already belonged to the local authorities and were in public use. Lancaster's Bailrigg site and Warwick's site near Coventry were mainly farm-land, and Canterbury's consisted of farms bought by compulsory purchase. Lancaster and East Anglia have since doubled their acreage by buying adjacent plots, and of the Seven only York, having added marginally to its 190 acres, is still close to the 200 minimum required by the UGC. The total floor space built in each university by 1970 averages slightly less than a million square feet, and in most cases is contained within a compact fraction of the total site.

The choice of architect came in every instance after the choice of the site, and by a most arbitrary process. The Academic Planning Board's recommendation was passed on to the UGC, and in this way seven consultant architects of distinction embarked on seven plans, with continuous consultation with their clients, but little mutual co-operation. Sir Basil Spence, the first to be chosen, for Sussex, already had experience of university building, as had the Architects' Co-Partnership. Certain distinguished names, such as Sir Leslie Martin, Sir Hugh Casson, and Philip Dowson, all hard at work in Oxford or Cambridge, were omitted, as were other teams like the Smithsons, who already had been energetically engaged in influential schemes for the older Civics.

The Leeds Development Plan of 1960 by Chamberlain, Powell and Bon was the first of its kind to tackle the study of a whole university environment, and was the origin of the concept of a 'ten-minute university'. Based on the amount of time wasted in walking about, this concept of a university in which it should not take more than ten minutes to walk from any one point to any other was quickly taken over by the seven new foundations, and most thoroughly examined in the Development Plan for York University, published in 1962 by Robert Mathew, Johnson-Marshall and Partners, after exhaustive discussions with the vice-chancellor. Although this report appeared after some of the early Spence buildings at Sussex had already been occupied, it was early enough to influence the designers of the environments at the other sites. Amongst the many principles it invoked was the development of a university which would give a sense of completeness from the earliest stage. It stressed the need for good communications between centres, but it could not be taken as a blueprint for the later master plans as the requirements of the clients were already diverging on many issues.

Perhaps the most important and irrevocable decision in planning was whether or not the university would be collegiate. It was a matter for each vice-chancellor and his Academic Planning Board: York, Kent, and Lancaster opted for collegiate structure, Sussex, East Anglia, Essex, and Warwick for a unitary basis.

Sir John Fulton at Sussex had felt that in order to compete with senior foundations on terms of intellectual equality, his university must remain a large but single unit. He did not want his Senior Common Room fragmented by the college system. This decision threw emphasis on the Schools of Studies as centres, and the buildings which were designed for them developed a social function as well. Lord James at York wanted to give the student a focus for loyalty and a point for identification with the university, a fixed focus at a time of rapid expansion. The college system did not need to drag with it from Oxford the associations of privilege, of exclusiveness, and of inequality. It could simply be an interdisciplinary social unit, with an optimum size well below that to which some of the academic departments would grow; a unit which would encompass teaching and research space as well as student residence within its own body.

A similar decision was taken by Dr. Templeman at Canterbury and Dr Carter at Lancaster. The 'collegiate decision', in which groups of people are not based on academic divisions but are *essentially* arbitrary, has a profound effect upon the architectural form of the university, yet the approaches of the architects concerned have nonetheless produced three totally different results.

Of the many implications of the college structure which are debated, one factor seems to be neglected. It is the further isolation of the Sciences. Science buildings are often special-purpose buildings, to house large machines or stand heavy loads. They are normally built on a different scale from residential or seminar teaching buildings and, quite apart from their horrifyingly rapid rate of obsolescence, are most economically built when out of direct contact with the other buildings. Thus the science student in a collegiate university gains less in terms of integration than the arts student, whose learning as well as whose living will take place in a college. At Sussex, with a single social centre, arts and science students go their separate ways to separate teaching buildings, but share social facilities equally.

An architect starting with a clean slate to design a university had little precedent, and the master plans which emerged were markedly individual. They are described in detail in later chapters under the separate universities. Apart from Kent and Warwick, they all have an organic pattern, and it is in the shape of the organism and the direction of growth that they differ most. They all, again apart from Kent, show a marked break with academic tradition in abandoning symmetrical and monumental forms, and allowing for a proliferation of buildings with a built-in flexibility to cope with the inevitable change of academic emphasis, and in this last respect the non-collegiate universities are at an advantage. The general trend, however (which can be seen in even more recent Robbins universities such as Bath and Surrey), is for tighter planning and greater compactness, with attention paid to the separation of pedestrians and vehicles. It is described by Michael Brawne in the Introduction to *University Planning and Design*, as 'the structuring of a system about a line, usually that of the main means of movement, open at both ends for further addition, and with activities attached to this line and growing outwards from it at right angles'.

Of the Seven, three universities have 'urban' master plans—East Anglia, Essex, and Lancaster. The system at Lancaster, designed by Shepheard and Epstein, fits Michael Brawne's definition perfectly. Perhaps it is appropriate to state here a personal preference for the new environment created at Lancaster amongst the Seven, but it is a preference shared with Sussex, much more arbitrary in plan but more successful in the superb aesthetic arrangement of buildings and the spaces between them.

3 Big Brother

'The quinquennial programme for which the UGC will be able to provide grant support must aggregate to a total programme for the country as a whole which is acceptable to the government.'

Here, spelled out in black and white in 'General Guidance on Quinquennial Planning, 1972–7', issued by the University Grants Committee to all universities in 1971,[1]* is a virtual declaration of centralised control, a statement which must impel vice-chancellors to wave goodbye to the traditional autonomy of the British university.

When the UGC was established in 1919 with the role of advising the government on university needs, its allocation of grants came to less than £700,000 in the first year, and accounted for just over a quarter of the income of the sixteen universities. By the academic year 1971–2 the Committee was distributing over £250,000,000 to forty-five institutions, and the contribution of the government finance, including student grants and money for research, had risen to over 90 per cent of the whole. These are the economic facts which accompany the increase in State participation in the university system, and according to Sir Sydney Caine, 'there is no pause in the growth of the effective share of government in the control of university policy'.[2]

The University Grants Committee interprets the needs of the universities to the government and vice versa, and has shouldered a much greater burden of responsibility since the Robbins Report, as more institutions have come under its wing. It consists overwhelmingly of academic members of the universities themselves, and is most anxious to avoid a we-and-they relationship with the universities, in spite of holding the purse strings for future and current development. Traditionally, vice-chancellors are not included on the Committee itself, and the importance of the independent Vice-Chancellors' Committee has grown as a response to the ever-increasing authority of the UGC.

The most important step towards centralised control came in 1966 when the Public Accounts Committee recommended that the Comptroller and Auditor General should have access to the universities' accounts, a recommendation which became operative in January 1968. Up to that date, university autonomy had included the right for each university to do what it liked with its government grant, without accountability. As the sum in question rose to approach 1 per cent of the national income, this situation was regarded as intolerable by the government in view of accountability in all other fields of public expenditure. As the instrument of the government, the UGC applied modern methods of economic analysis, and then took the extra responsibility of suggesting how many students the grants could efficiently train. The UGC has the aim of ensuring value for money. Unlike the original Big Brother, it is not seeking uniformity amongst the universities, but it is concerned

* The superior numbers throughout refer to the Bibliography.

about productivity and the avoidance of waste by overlapping effort or the under-use of facilities.

For a better understanding of the development of the new environments of the seven universities founded by the UGC, a brief explanation of the financial machinery is useful. Money reaches the university direct from the UGC in three different ways. Recurrent grants providing for salaries, maintenance, libraries and other running costs are based on five-yearly or quinquennial estimates for each university. The year 1972 marks the end of one quinquennium and the beginning of another. These grants are designed to ensure continuity, and since it is extremely difficult to anticipate needs five years ahead, a certain measure of flexibility is built into the system to allow for increased salaries and inflation in running costs (the Brown Index). Universities are in competition with one another in making their own estimates, and in order to ensure a satisfactory slice of the cake must put up a good case for themselves based on student numbers. Non-recurrent grants are for the provision of new buildings and sites and furnishings, and assume a much larger proportion of the total in the new universities, which had to start from scratch, than in the long-established ones. The Seven had each spent over £6,000,000 of Treasury money in the period up to 1970. The third source of direct funds is a separate grant related to the number of students in the university, for the provision and renewal of equipment, and comprises about 7 per cent of the total.

The dovetailing of a recurrent grant, estimated for up to five years before it is used, with a capital development scheme operated on a year-to-year basis is an intricate exercise, especially in a period of rising inflation. A major building takes a period of at least three or four years from the time the clients supply the architect with a brief to the occupation of the building, and so a system of phasing of buildings is adopted, unofficially related to the quinquennial estimates, and to make matters more complicated, is based on a three-year term to allow for the necessary gestation process. At the time of writing most of the Seven are concluding building programmes to coincide with the end of the quinquennium in 1972, and all have established building programmes for the period up to 1976, after a dialogue with the UGC. These are largely putative in the absence of specific government commitment on finance for the next five years, which is especially disconcerting for those universities whose master plans were developed as long-range projects.

In view of the progressive contraction of funds with inflation, it would at first seem that the universities amongst the Seven which got started early and are well advanced in building have an advantage, but this advantage is modified by the establishment of norms.

Norms have been developed by the UGC from detailed information of available facilities and the usage of accommodation, and the effect of the comparative statistics can be put brutally simply as follows: a university which has above-average facilities for, say, language teaching, can expect in future *below* average contributions for the extension of these facilities, with the result that more students will be employing the facilities more intensively, and the initial advantage of spaciousness or whatever will be lost. A levelling-up of facilities is the object of the exercise, but to the individual universities and their architects it means unexpected strains in unexpected places.

Financially, the Seven were all given the same start in life, they were treated as equals by the UGC and their targets were the same. There have subsequently been penalties for extra-rapid growth. At present, only a substantial increase in student numbers brings an assurance of capital grants for new building, and if there were a university among the Seven which wished to stand still, to mark time or to take a breath, the presence of the norms denies it the opportunity to do so, for it will be expected to house and educate the number of students indicated by its 'norms rating'. The government is insisting on larger numbers of graduates at ever lower cost, and the help of the universities has been sought by the UGC on investigating the fuller usage of non-specialised teaching space, and even the possibility of re-time-tabling the university year so that students work a shift system, using facilities for up to forty-eight weeks a year instead of thirty. It is certainly wasteful for specialised teaching buildings such as Physics laboratories to be used for only three-fifths of the year. Such buildings are expensive to build—more so than seminar rooms for arts-based graduates—part of the reason why it costs a third as much again to train a science graduate as an arts man. Unfortunately, the science disciplines, the most expensive to house and equip, are those which most rapidly go obsolete. Libraries are also expensive, and can only be saved from the same fate if they are carefully planned, as indicated in Chapter 5.

Ironically, the most permanent requirement in the Seven is residential accommodation, which is the least expensive building to provide but the one which the UGC finds most difficult to finance. The intention to contribute only marginally to the cost of residences, to avoid giving the new universities an unfair advantage over the older Civics, took vice-chancellors by surprise, especially those whose collegiate conceptions depended on an integration of residential and teaching facilities. The UGC has been flexible in this matter and now contributes fixed sums to the loan-financed schemes described in the next chapter, but buildings for residence have depended heavily from the start on donated funds, and in particular the university appeals fund money.

Each of the Seven launched appeals, and most were able to finance about 20 per cent of their buildings in the first five years from this private source, averaging £1,000,000 per university. Lancaster, thanks to a single gift of £500,000 from the County, has been able to spend over £2,000,000 on specialised buildings without the need for UGC approval or contributions, but the new universities in less industrial areas, such as Kent and Essex, have had a more modest response to their appeals. In any case, the steam tends to go out of such funds as the novelty of the foundation wears off, and the campuses must expect to revert to a greater dependence on the government for their capital expenditure.

A comparison between running costs and capital costs underlines the relative cheapness of the architecture in the Seven, even though buildings inevitably cost more than recurrent expenditure in the first few years. By 1971–2 an average of £1,500,000 was spent by each of the Seven on all running expenses and the annual cost per student has been stabilised at around £900—no more than at traditional universities. Value judgements of the importance of the visual environment must inevitably be made in the long term, and many benefits simply cannot be estimated. But the buildings are intended to last, and taken over a sixty-year period the total of building costs should be a low percentage of expenditure as a whole. The buildings, if they are flexible, pay for themselves over and over again.

In addition to State support direct and indirect by way of student fees, private income and fees for research can help the universities in a small way to balance their budgets.

An obvious private source of revenue is the conference trade which is wooed for the vacations, when student accommodation and lecture hall space are taken over for short periods profitable to the universities. Some more recent university achitects have taken suitability for conferences into their general planning brief—an unfortunate step since the temporary expedient in a time of financial stringency may turn out to be a fashion of short duration, whilst its whims will be imprinted permanently upon the university's design.

Two major financial events have affected the development of the seven campuses. Firstly, the financial pause in 1965 which delayed buildings and affected some universities badly. Secondly, the major cutbacks announced in 1968 which left all growing universities wondering what their future would hold, only five years after the imaginative period of their foundation.

In the move to lower the cost of learning, or at least the unit-cost of higher education, buildings, like everything else, have to suffer. Any special pleading for architecture must take into consideration the need to resist the erosion of other benefits such as the student-staff ratio, currently 8·5 : 1 and the best in the world (compared with 30 : 1 in France and 12 : 1 in the United States), but likely to rise to 9 : 1 or more in the next few years.

The real danger to the physical environment in striving for greater economic efficiency lies not in the reduction of the opportunity to build, but in the acceptance of a progressively lower standard of buildings to cope with the required growth in numbers. Accommodation of a more temporary nature would be costly in the long term, and would bring about a sad levelling-out of the campuses which have so far had such encouragement from the UGC to develop their individuality.

4 Residences

'A shortage of residential accommodation could become the biggest single bottleneck in the years ahead.' The University Grants Committee Report in 1970 recognised a problem, but could make no promises about the provision of finance to solve it.

Without accommodation, for university staff of all kinds as well as for students, there can be no university. Students need little encouragement to live away from home, and come as immigrants to the new university region, and it would have been irresponsible to found any of the Seven without considering the impact on the local community of at least 5,000 university dependents within the first ten years. One of the UGC's first requirements for a new university foundation was therefore a local guarantee that satisfactory lodgings would be available. However, the actual choice of locations implied a total impact of between 1·5 per cent (Warwick) and 15 per cent (Canterbury) on the community, and the latter figure is much more than a town can house with ease.

The York Development Plan of 1962 laid great stress on the need to provide appropriate residence for teaching and administrative staff, as well as students, and at all the six foundations which followed Sussex the intention was clearly that the university was to be highly residential in character. The collegiate/unitary decision greatly influenced the *kind* of residence intended but not the magnitude of the problem.

The living environment is vital to the individual student, and a satisfactory on-campus arrangement can be vitiated by an unsatisfactory arrangement within the town, with student ghettoes or, even worse, isolated individuals. Time wasted in bus queues and the depression of a miserable bed-sitter can be a more permanent memory than a good room in college, and most of the Seven have tackled the lodgings problem with energy.

Keele University, which was totally residential for the first fifteen years, adopted the traditional Hall of Residence for students of the same sex, recommended in 1956 by the Niblett Report on Student Residence.[8] By the time Sussex University was founded this concept was already falling from favour. It was also most expensive since it had to provide central lounges for recreation, dining rooms and catering facilities which were invariably used well below capacity, as anyone who has spent time in a student Hall knows. Sussex adopted a 'boarding out' system for first-year students in selected boarding houses in Brighton, and built four units of accommodation on the university campus, each to house about 120 students. Taking the form of low blocks with corridors of rooms and small shared kitchens, these were tentative steps towards providing the student with a greater degree of personal freedom, but

◁ *4. Student study bedrooms at York University. This wing of Langwith College, built in prefabricated* CLASP, *abuts onto the artificial lake.*

in their quadrangular and inward-looking design still carried the overtones of the academic 'college' without the common social life.

The collegiate universities tackled the problem of residence differently: teaching, social and residential areas were closely integrated at York, Kent, and Lancaster. At Kent, in particular, compact units brought students close together in single-sex corridors of eight people at a time, with a more formal dining arrangement and large common rooms, library and working areas within the college. In the early colleges, all residential facilities for students were of an identical standard, and non-residential members of the college were given a foothold, or at least a locker key, which was intended to help to inspire loyalty. Here, as at York and Lancaster, an economy is made when certain facilities such as college refectories and social areas are used both during the working day and in the evening. It was the intention that students should easily be able to take advantage of the opportunities the college provides for mixing, whilst at the same time retaining a sense of privacy. The corridors are so tucked away that no one will intrude, but the student has only got to leave the corridor to be back in the swim. In York, residential students are housed in wings of the asymmetrical colleges, study-bedrooms often close to teaching rooms and seminar rooms. Similarly, in the early colleges at Lancaster it is difficult to see where teaching ends and dwelling begins. The mixing of teaching and living elements is an essential characteristic of the collegiate system. The UGC student numbers recommendations for 1972–7 pose special problems for the college universities. If more students are taken in without the provision of finance for new colleges, the existing ones have to grow new residential limbs, as has happened in Oxford and in Cambridge, where St John's College is a good example, thus changing their character and scale. Otherwise, detached residential blocks have to be built, which upsets the collegiate concept.

Warwick University chose to build so-called student 'Halls' which are really no more than dense blocks of study bedrooms, with common washing and cooking facilities for groups of sixteen. A social building for the first 'Hall' at some slight distance from the blocks is much like a Students' Union, as it has had to serve this purpose for the whole university. Architects generally strive to conceal the shortcomings involved in building student residences on a strict budget, but most of these, such as lack of privacy, uniformity in furnishing and an appearance of overcrowding, are embarrassingly on show at Warwick.

Uniformity was an intention at Essex, but the chosen formula—high-rise urban housing with students in flats of up to sixteen individuals—is the most uncompromising of all. Up to 1972 there were no on-campus alternatives, only a fifty-fifty chance of being more than half-way up a tower. Apart from Lancaster with a single tower, Essex is the only university to have made use of high buildings as part of its general experiment in urban living. Towers are of course expensive to build and to service, and of the original twenty-two which were planned only six have been built. Marie Clossick wrote a thorough sociological study of life in the towers in 1966, but the environment at Essex gave her no basis for comparison as there were no alternative residences, and the towers were very much a novelty at that time. The possibilities of students happening to meet in a high building are few, as the community is sliced up into horizontal layers which share only a common lift. The residential situa-

5. Essex University stood the Niblett Report on student residence on its end, and instead of 'cosy halls' built four tower blocks for 200 students each.

tion at Essex was complicated in the early days by experimental combinations of study-bedrooms for residents and study facilities for living-out students; it did not produce the desired result of integrating the community but rather a 'weather cottage' situation in which residents went out as non-residents came in, and this experiment has now been abandoned.

A 'modulus' of twelve students comprises the unit for on-campus residence at East Anglia, five such groups living in each of a series of small compact blocks. As at Essex and Warwick, the sub-unit occupies a floor and shares cooking and washing facilities. There is the same complaint about over-exposure as at Warwick, but the residential terraces, described in Chapter 9, have such glamour that students cannot complain that living there is a dull experience. Interconnection between the blocks themselves is informal, with access at two levels, and a balance between major units and sub-units exists which is unique in the seven new universities. There are two other forms of residential accommodation at East Anglia, the Waveney terraces and the 'Z' block, which are referred to later; these should not be confused with the more imaginative terraces of Denys Lasdun.

All seven universities have some provision for shared rooms amongst the purpose-built blocks, but single rooms are much more popular, and greatly in the majority.

All the original residential accommodation in the Seven was financed wholly or partly from the individual university appeal funds, with specific donations for residential buildings at Warwick and later at Lancaster. The UGC was persuaded to make some contributions at the collegiate universities. In the telescoped evolution at the new universities, the results of the methods adopted by the different foundations and described above can be called the first generation of student residence.

The second generation did not emerge until the funds ran dry. Based on borrowed capital, the second type is widely known as the 'Lancaster Scheme' after the university which pioneered it in 1967. It is loan-financed student housing consisting essentially of new residences which must generate enough income to pay back the original capital loan and interest in the same way as a private house-owner pays back his mortgage. Such a system is circumscribed by the prevailing rates of interest, the cost of building to minimum acceptable standards, and the amount which the student can reasonably be expected to pay from his grant. Normal market forces should keep all three in balance, but in 1971 they had become so far out of line that loan-financed student housing schemes had to be temporarily shelved. The economic handicap of the system is of course that income is basically rent for thirty-six weeks residence a year, supplemented by vacation lettings, compared with fifty-two weeks rent on normal residential property.

The practical disadvantages are firstly the need to design buildings which require the absolute minimum of maintenance—such as repainting, and even cleaning—lest an increase in maintenance costs through the years throws out the delicate financial balance, and secondly the need to design housing which would be suitable for family housing and private sale, since the lenders, be they banks or building societies, insist that the property should be saleable if the university policy is changed or if the universities ceased to meet their commitments.

A university suffers in this respect when the campus is a long way out of town, for the suitability for private housing increases with the proximity to urban centres. But the cost of urban sites would overwhelm such a project, and the universities are in the fortunate position of having their own campus land free of charge.

Up to 1971, three of the Seven had successfully instituted loan-financed schemes, Lancaster and Sussex on the campus, and East Anglia both on the campus and at a student residence centre five miles away. The strict financial limits and careful costing of these schemes have been of the greatest benefit in concentrating study on students' requirements ('financial stringency, like the prospect of being hanged, concentrates the mind wonderfully', writes David Crease in 'The Student in Residence', *Architectural Review*, April 1970). An interesting and appropriate housing solution need not be a very expensive one, but unfortunately the concentration on the building of a residential block for an ever-lower per capita figure has meant a lowering of certain standards and a descending norm of quality. The UGC announced in 1970 that it would contribute 25 per cent (roughly £250) per student to future loan-based housing schemes, towards furnishing and capital costs. This assistance does not make loan-financed schemes viable owing to high interest rates, and pressure is growing for an allocation of a pool of government capital at low interest through the UGC, to provide student housing irrespective of prevailing market rates.

The architects' briefing on the individual living requirements of the student has changed little in the last decade (since the publication of the Parker Morris Report on housing in general). The size of rooms has shrunk from the more spacious Lindsay Halls at Keele to an average of about 120 square feet per student, and whatever the *form* of residence, the size of the sub-groups sharing common facilities in on-campus residences has varied between eight and twenty. The importance of this sub-group as a 'household' or 'family' varies according to the social structure around it—collegiate or otherwise—but somewhere between these two figures is a satisfactory social unit size for people of the same age, state of health, and roughly the same interests and

6. *In Denys Lasdun's Terraces at East Anglia the arrangement of the rooms on each level is V-shaped, students sharing the 'breakfast room' at the point of the 'V'.*

7, 8. *A wide-angle lens takes in the full width of a student's room (left) in the Waveney Terrace at East Anglia, and also the full range of its furnishings. Walls are left unplastered, windows uncurtained. 400 students live in rooms in two stark blocks, and these numbers will be doubled in 1972. In Rootes Hall (opposite), at Warwick University, 500 students live in two terrace blocks, one for men and one for women, separated by a concrete path and rose bushes. The high density of life here is communicated by the exterior, with its glowering windows and graph-paper regularity.*

needs. An important development in the facilities shared by these 'households' is the increasing emphasis on the kitchen and cooking facilities to cope with the rise in self-catering by students. The tiny pantry-cabins in the Park Houses at Sussex, in the early colleges at Kent and the under-equipped 'breakfast' rooms in the Lasdun terraces at East Anglia contrast with the spacious kitchens in the new Essex towers, in the Park Village at Sussex and on the ground floor of the new low-rise housing for Bath University. The change in the role of the kitchens from a place to boil an egg to a room in which to throw a party can be seen at Kent, as the third and fourth colleges were built with increasingly spacious kitchen and social facilities for 'households'. The collegiate universities have more opportunity for comparing different arrangements. At Warwick, alteration of existing structures has turned eating areas into attractive places for students to linger after meals. In the East Anglia terraces, the experience of cauliflower cheese made in the kettle and the toaster used for heating baked beans indicated clearly that the attractive 'breakfast' rooms were in demand as proper kitchens, and needed less spartan services. These modifications are now being made.

Many students' rooms have their own wash-basins, but this is not universally popular as they take up space and can be unattractive if they are near the entrance to the room (as at Kent) and not shut away in a cupboard (as at York). The centralised washing facilities are a great source of noise, especially when placed at the core of the building as in Rootes Hall, Warwick. The sound insulation, ventilation, heating, and furnishing are all matters of intimate concern to the student and the seven universities have not been backward in asking students to specify their requirements. There is a constant stream of criticism from users concerning all these matters and the factor most neglected is obviously sound insulation. Good sound insulation is expensive, and when it is present it is not noticed, like the absence of a headache. Certainly it is invisible and money spent on it *appears* to be wasted. The lack of good sound insulation is a major cause of social friction within the 'households' and a positive reason for a student to feel that he lives in a 'flimsy' unreal environment.

The lack of privacy involved in sound transmission and in windows which overlook one another is inevitable when temporary buildings are commandeered for residences, like the Nissen huts at Horsham airfield used for first-year students at East Anglia, but a major factor for consideration in the planning of purpose-built student residential blocks. The overglazing of student rooms is criticised at Sussex (Park Village), Warwick (Rootes Hall) and East Anglia (the Lasdun terraces), and curtains or posters placed over lower window panels indicate the need for opaque or translucent panels when floor-to-ceiling glazing is an essential part of the structure.

Close-carpeting in student rooms greatly aids sound absorption (as do acoustic ceiling tiles) and this carpeting is often cheaper in maintenance than a combination of tiles and rugs. Maximum storage space in rooms is vital and the bed, which may occupy up to a fifth of the floor area, often has useful cupboards underneath. Bookshelves, desks and reading lamps are standard requirements, and by standardising purchases furnishing can be significantly cheapened. But every student wants to be able to give his room individuality, and identical furnishings and curtains do not help in this respect. Bolting to the wall, as in the East Anglia Waveney terrace, further reduces costs—for example, it reduces the number of legs a table needs—but it savagely restricts the occupant's freedom to make the room his own. In the loan-financed Waveney terraces it is almost restricted to what he cares to pin up on the bolted-to-the-wall pinboard. In the Essex towers, furniture bolted to a rail around the room can be rearranged in a number of ways, a feature which many of the students obviously appreciate.

The Essex towers and the single tower at Lancaster are alone in the new universities in providing access by lift. Housing is limited to four storeys in all the other new universities and often access is by a staircase tower. The 'staircase princple' was suggested by Frank Thistlethwaite of East Anglia when considering the social environment, but in most places the sub-units consist of horizontal layers like large flats. Only in the most recent developments have the sub-units been separated from one another vertically. In the Park Village (plate 28) at Sussex, the 'staircases' of twelve students are arranged like terraced houses lining the pedestrian 'street' between them. These units of twelve have two kitchens, on ground floor and second floor, and bath and shower facilities in between. Similar 'vertical' divisions are found in the residential accommodation at the technological universities of Bath and Loughborough. At Bath, intercommunication from one 'staircase' to the next is by an external covered way, each 'stair' having its own front door. If the stairs are only going to be used by the members of the staircase themselves and their visitors, they can be brought more intimately to the common area of the household, with some saving of space and expense. At Bath the design of the housing is by the consultant architects Robert Mathew, Johnson-Marshall and Partners; at Sussex it was by Hughes, Lomax and Adutt, part of a package deal—a 'design and build' tender—from the local firm of Kier Ltd. Construction in brick and creosoted wood was designed to harmonise with the rest of the campus and the Park Village has now been extended to a population of about 700 individuals—enough to support a shop and a pub. Another village may be created elsewhere in the park.

Another 'design and build' contract was made between the University of East Anglia and Laing for the notorious 'Z' block. Originally designed to meet an urgent need for accommodation at a low price, it made no attempt to create student communities, simply to house students as economically as possible. It was built away from the main site at Horsham St Faith, on the airfield which already housed most of the first-year students.

Existing officers' and airmen's quarters at Horsham were converted into women's and men's study-bedrooms as a matter of expediency in 1964. The resulting accommodation is far below the usual standard of purpose-built blocks, and much criticised as noisy and draughty. 'I arrived late at night, in a special coach,' said one student. 'I thought the place looked rather like a barracks. I was surprised next morning to find it really was one.' Most students at East Anglia remember the bleak and windy environment of their first year with some horror, because of its remoteness both from the town (four miles) and the university (five miles), yet when pressed, they often agree that they were very happy living in the Horsham barracks, and it is interesting that they will readily criticise the more intriguing purpose-built Lasdun terraces on the university plain, while making allowances for Horsham because it was a conversion. There is no student objection to living in converted property.

There has been much activity in the conversion of property close to the seven campuses, both privately and by the universities themselves. The price of building land makes purpose-built housing within the town uneconomic, but the York design unit headed by David Crease has made a thorough study of the purchase and renovation of existing property, and in a pilot scheme has converted four properties with great skill and success. York University has also converted a nurses' home for residence for eighty-nine students. Warwick University has several university houses in Coventry, Leamington and Kenilworth. The University of East Anglia houses twenty students in a large house in Norwich, and the University of Kent plans to convert Hothe Court for a similar number. This sort of piecemeal conversion, though often providing the most satisfactory living environment, is dependent on property values and a steady flow of appropriate houses on to the market. It is not easy to finance, and could never keep pace unassisted with the demand for student accommodation. At Sussex, where property values are particularly high, the

9. *Clustering together at the eastern end of Cartmel College, Lancaster, are the residential units of the famous loan-financed Lancaster Scheme. Seven of the blocks share common walls but do not intercommunicate, and each block, housing 32 students, has its own entrance. Similar units have now been built for Furness College and Fylde College on the same campus.*

total student population nears 10,000 when the Polytechnic and College of Education students are added to the university students. The abundance of accommodation in 1959 has rapidly changed to a serious dearth, with rents rising out of reach, and the local council is anxious to see a higher proportion of students housed on the campus (40 per cent) to relieve some of the pressure in the town. A scheme for converting a large Brighton hotel for student residence has so far failed to attract sponsors.

The mounting demand for student residences and the accumulation of data by the UGC may lead shortly to a firm policy on design. It is essential that the individuality of residence design is assured and that a blueprint for residences is avoided. The UGC can and does offer advice on student residences but it often appears that the initiative is left too much with the architect, and the same mistakes are repeated over and over again.

The fashionable policy of providing identical facilities for all may be replaced by one in which the sizes of rooms (and rents) within a sub-unit vary considerably. Some students are quite content with small rooms, others vitally need room to expand in, to store things in, and to be noisy in. The housing designed by Haydn Smith of Taylor Young and Partners at Lancaster (plate 9) attractively provides several different options within its economical plan, and at the same time by means of its irregular ground plan a series of small and intimate façades which help to give the individual student confidence in the individuality of his own corner of the university. This design provides one of the major touchstones for future development.

5 The Design of Libraries

Armed with £175,000 each for the purchase of books, the librarians of the seven new universities were faced with the task of building from scratch a well-balanced collection relating directly to the academic plans of the university. Each librarian's problem would vary according to whether or not the university perhaps emphasised law, with its very high bibliographical demands, or chemistry, with its needs for backruns of vast numbers of periodicals, but all had one common problem: that of developing a worthwhile library of books at an unprecedented speed. They would also have a brand new building to house the collection, and the opportunity of influencing its design.

A library is a unique building which cannot be used for anything else. Its planning has been the subject of a great deal of research, and the way in which it has been tackled has varied considerably over the ages. American university planners insist on a library consultant to act as a catalyst between architect and librarian in the interpretation of needs in this very specialised field, where undesired features can easily be frozen for ever into the plan. The Parry Report on Libraries for the UGC in 1967 recommended a similar system for Britain, but the seven very different plans in the seven new universities had arisen from a dialogue of direct consultation between librarian and architect. In the germinal work on library design, *Planning Academic and Research Libraries*, Keyes Metcalf draws attention to a continuing problem: 'Libraries . . . have never found a satisfactory way of preventing or even slowing up the growth in library space requirements.' One of the most embarrassing manifestations of this is the way in which famous libraries such as the British Museum have to house parts of their collections in makeshift and unsatisfactory accommodation because their own imposing buildings are no longer adequate for needs.

The librarians at the new universities did not have to carry the burden of an archaic and inadequate building of historic and architectural interest, such as the Bodleian in Oxford. Some of the traditional problems of new library architecture were also absent—such as the accommodation of existing (and perhaps obsolete) collections and the incorporation of existing usage patterns and bulky furniture—and all their libraries had the advantage of a high order of priority on the buildings list. Librarians and architects simply had to avoid the trap of designing a building which would become out of date quickly. A new library building which is perfectly adapted to its needs on the day it opens can be a dismal failure a decade later if it has not made provision for expansion and change. E. R. S. Fifoot, librarian of Edinburgh University, commenting in 1968, said, 'few recent [library] buildings, if any, have shown in their planning any awareness that change is the only constant factor'.[4]

◁ *10. One of the four high reading halls in the library at Kent.*

With the ever-increasing amount of published information, the average growth rate of a university library stock is about 5 per cent a year. In a *new* university it is, of course, vastly greater, and after eight years a library of 200,000 volumes is still increasing at the rate of about 25,000 books a year. With five hundred new books arriving every week, the library has to have a capacity to house and make available this increase in stock. Vast storage vaults are inappropriate as all the Seven have adopted the open-access principle as by far the most efficient and economical method of bringing readers and books together. Six of the Seven have solved the problem of rapid growth over the first few years by designing a library to be built in phases. Of these six, Sussex and Lancaster have already completed their third phase, and the odd one out, Warwick, built a big library in one phase which would house teaching departments on the upper floors until the space was needed.

To solve the long-term problems of expansion at an unknown rate, it is essential that the library building has space around it to expand into. If it is hemmed in by other buildings it is obviously going to be impossible to maintain the physical continuity of a single building. However, it is important that a centralised library—as an organ vital to all departments—should have a situation near the heart of the campus, something which is at odds with the need for space for expansion. All the Seven have left some room for expansion, although at Kent and East Anglia it will largely be filled when Stage Two is built; these two universities and Essex already show at one end of their libraries the raw blind walls to which their siamese twins will be attached.

The principal requirement in new library design is flexibility. This is defined by Fifoot as 'the interchangeability, not overnight but over the summer vacation, of all major stack areas, reading areas and staff areas'. Undoubtedly the system of building which best answers this need is the modular system, in which the weight of the structure is carried by columns built at regular distances apart, and not by internal walls. Partition walls can easily be rearranged inside such a structure, which is adopted by all the Seven except for Kent. The average size of the module is 22 feet, although it varies from 25 feet down to 18 and it is often broken into smaller sub-units, as at East Anglia and York, for windows and, of course, for book stacks, which average 3 feet in length.

If floor areas are to be available for book stacks as well as other less weighty purposes, then a load-bearing strength of 130 to 150 pounds per square foot is necessary, creating a higher initial cost but contributing to the flexibility. Interchangeability of book stacks and reading area in the seven new universities varies between about 60 per cent and 75 per cent of the floor area as a whole. The UGC recommendations allow for a 40 per cent 'balance' of space, not used for readers or books, and incidentally recommend about 25 square feet of space per reader. Staircases and lift shafts, plumbing and other services, whilst capable of being moved within a modular structure, are in practice permanent features of a library interior, and are often sensibly grouped close together so that, although excluded from the flexible areas, they represent a single internal island. They are areas of heavy circulation and are therefore potentially noisy. In some library plans, as at Essex and Kent, they are located at a far corner of the building, although in both cases this location will become more central when the next stage is built.

The flexibility requirement and the modular system which delivers it are

11. *A monumental casket for learning. Lord Holford's library at Kent stands conspicuously on top of the hill facing Canterbury. The final design will be symmetrical.*

most sensibly accommodated within a square or rectangular ground plan. Irregular-shaped plans, which offer greater opportunities for inventiveness by the architect, have not been used by any one of the Seven and this is partly in the interests of economy. Some of the other basic needs of a new library are ease of access to books and index, with the minimum of movement to reduce internal traffic and distraction, adequate and varied reading space and a centralised control for the issuing and processing of book loans.

The traditional concept of a library as a monumental casket of learning, set apart and rather daunting, dies hard among architects and the progression from the dignified but aloof building on a podium to the central, inconspicuous and informal one follows a rough chronological sequence amongst the Seven. The libraries of Sussex, York, Essex, and Kent stand high and proud on their campus, though both Sussex and Kent are fairly central. East Anglia, Warwick, and Lancaster are easier to approach, and Lancaster (the only one not to be designed by the architect of the master plan) is particularly central, warm and welcoming.

The library at Sussex, overwhelmingly the most heavily used, is also the largest. As more and more books are bought, more space is required for book stacks, administration and cataloguing and, like a crab inside its shell, conditions get very much worse before they suddenly get better as the library moves into a newly completed phase. At Sussex the number of reading spaces had to be reduced from 850 to 580 as more books came piling in and space was taken up for administration and issuing in anticipation of the completion of the third phase. Suddenly, in February 1971, the library space was almost doubled and both books (over 300,000) and readers (with 1,100 places) could breathe more easily.

The much later library at Kent (Stage One opened in 1968) is the most

traditional of the Seven. Plans for its extension, which would make it perfectly symmetrical about its spacious entrance hall, are ensnared by the escalation of building costs and the inflexibility of the architect's plan. Stage One has four high reading halls, each occupying two storeys and flanking a long spine of book stacks. Readers filter through the stacks to the halls so there is no routeway of dense circulation, and the halls themselves, beautifully furnished, are an excellent place to work. To build Stage Two to the same pattern, however, would be extravagant of space, and plans have gone ahead to modify it internally so that it will have single-storey reading areas interchangeable with book stacks spread across the full width of the building, whilst the exterior will retain the monumental windows of Stage One and keep aesthetic unity.

Much more drastic rethinking about expansion will take place at York, where the design includes several basic mistakes and a lot of waste space. A central well, like a deep swimming pool or a nuclear reactor tank (plate 12) causes distraction to readers and accentuates noise, but cannot be floored over as it is integral to the ventilation system. It will not be repeated in Stage Two. Unfortunately, the module for the window mullions, internal walls and light wells is out of phase with the module for the column supports, so that concrete pillars crop up at awkward places, impairing circulation.

Both Essex and Warwick have built libraries six storeys high. At Warwick, as at York, access to books begins at first floor level, the ground floor being taken up with library administration and the book shop. At Essex, the student must climb two floors before coming to books, although his journey to the upper levels is eased by the famous paternoster lift which, like an oval ferris wheel, hoists open-sided cabins continuously up and down. Rather terrifying for the uninitiated, it is most efficient at delivering large numbers of people to wherever they want to go, and will still be adequate when the library has doubled in size. Both Warwick and Essex have largely peripheral reading areas, with shared tables and central dividers. They also have extensive glazing and, being high, interesting views: Essex seems almost to have been designed as a building to look out from.

The library at East Anglia also stands six floors high, but access is at the level of the elevated walkway, which means that administration and servicing occupy the central (and entrance) two floors of the sandwich, and separate arts subjects on the upper floors from science subjects on the lower ones. Like Essex and Warwick, it is heavily glazed, but deep concrete fins restrict the amount of sun coming in and the view looking out, and divide the periphery of the building into secluded bays.

In Lancaster, most of the glazing surrounds the four sides of an internal courtyard, stepped back at each level and used for outdoor reading in summer. The external walls are not heavily glazed, and from the exterior the building is quite self-effacing. With a small entrance squeezed between the university bookshop and coffee bar, it also neatly solves the problem of refreshment. Internal coffee rooms with machine dispensers, as at Sussex and East Anglia, are dreary and smoky. To have no refreshment room, as at Kent, is maddening, especially if it is raining. A coffee shop at the exit from the library is an

◁ *12. In the deep central well of the library at York, modifications have been made to dampen sound. A suspended canopy (lower left) reduces noise from the issuing desk below it, and a second 'skin' on the ceiling now quietens the rain which drums on the fibreglass roof.*

asset which increases the efficiency of the building, and one is found at York as well.

In library design, the proper functioning of the building includes its suitability as a place to work in, particularly for the undergraduate who, unlike professors, probably has nowhere else quiet to go to. Matters such as noise level, visual distraction, draughts and physical discomfort fully deserve to be considered as fundamental problems.

The furnishings in the libraries of the Seven are of a high standard. Options in seating arrangements range from private lockable carrels, available at all Seven but usually for postgraduates, through waist-high cabins (at Warwick), individual seats with dividers on three sides (most common at Kent, Sussex, and Lancaster), to tables with central divisions or no divisions at all. It is essential to provide variety and the opportunity for some students to tuck themselves away in seclusion whilst others can spread out books and maps over large tables when there are few readers about. Perhaps it is at East Anglia, where the furnishings were designed and chosen by the architect, Denys Lasdun, that the most relaxed and spacious atmosphere is achieved, and the level of usage is accordingly high. Light-coloured wood in the furnishings here, as at Kent and Sussex, helps to make the library a welcoming place.

13, 14. Designed for privacy, interlocking booths (above) in the library at Lancaster University surround the reader on three sides with mahogany. Sunlight streams through the net curtains of the windows facing onto an internal courtyard where readers can take books in fine weather. In the reading area of the library at East Anglia (left) are spacious tables, some with central divisions, and the deep structural 'fins' on the external walls provide study pockets down the library sides.

At the Seven, most reading places are individually lit, and by fluorescent strips. Book stacks are best kept away from sunny windows and are illuminated by strip lights in the ceiling. These are efficient if at right angles to the stacks but likely to cause shadows if parallel, and the best solution is at Essex, where a metal grid allows them to be rearranged in any position.

Most of the Seven have to house special collections with special demands, such as the Redlich Library and the Ford Railway Collection at Lancaster, the Sir Edward Coke Library at East Anglia and the Lloyd George Library at Kent. Unfortunately, nothing is standard about the size of material to be stored, and nothing is sure about its shape and size in the future. Huge books, microfilms, records and tapes cannot be housed on the normally adaptable metal shelves, and each university tackles these problems in its own way. The storing of periodicals, however, is particularly important and centralised facilities for current and recent issue storage, together with reader space, has produced some of the most imaginative and attractive working areas in the libraries. The periodical room at Kent, above the main entrance, is a very good example. Of course, periodicals are frequently wanted for consultation in the teaching departments, and many science departments (for example, Chemistry at Sussex) have special libraries for periodicals.

15. The ceiling grid in the Essex library allows the lights to be moved easily if the book stacks and study areas are rearranged.

The argument for and against centralised facilities does not rest only on the economies of avoiding duplication of stock but also on accessibility. Nothing is more frustrating than to be locked out of the casket of learning, or turned out ten minutes before closing time, with nowhere else to read. A library building which can open for long hours, seven days a week throughout term is essential. In this respect the collegiate universities of York and Kent have an advantage, for each college has a small internal library with a limited (sometimes hilariously small) book stock, but reading facilities open twenty-four hours a day. The 'gatehouse' block at Warwick serves a similar function, for it is a cluster of small reading rooms outside the main check-out of the library proper, and can be used by students out of library hours. The rooms are beautifully furnished and the facilities most valuable.

A great many students from the civic universities confess to never having used their libraries, and the fault is not theirs alone. Libraries can be deathly, depressing, dark and cold, and the business of learning will be shabbily accomplished in such a setting. Students at the Seven will never experience the trauma of contact with reference books in this way, for they can read in comfort and space. The seven new libraries have no traditions to demolish, only the uncertainty of the future to contend with, and being built in stages, they should be able to learn from their own mistakes.

6 The New and the Less New

'Do you want to go to a campus university,' said the careers lecturer, 'or to a city university?' The audience, at a careers course in 1969, was a privileged one. A decade earlier, the question—if it had been asked at all—would have been 'Do you prefer Oxbridge or Redbrick?', and the great majority would have opted for the former, on the basis of its status, both intellectual and otherwise. With certain independently-minded exceptions, the cream went to Oxbridge, if they could get there.

The Robbins Committee urged a diversion of emphasis from Oxford and Cambridge, and these two universities have barely grown whilst total numbers of students have doubled.

The development of the campus environment, not only in the Seven, is the external manifestation of the decade of expansion. It represents an Americanisation of university life for the British student, for the campuses, like American colleges, are total environments. When you leave your lecture room, go shopping, visiting or even walking, you are still in the university and you are not necessarily in contact with any other kind of life.

The policy of expansion in this particular way means that British campuses have developed so fast that they are now visited and studied by university planners from America. There is also interest from Europe where, apart from the Scandinavian countries, increased numbers have largely been packed into existing city universities. This is the second time in recent years that an architectural solution for education has attracted attention, for the post-war schools-building programme was revolutionary and much praised. In an emergency situation, a system for secondary schools was produced and built with only minor variations across the country. The English achievement in building schools is recognised everywhere, although the visitor might find himself whisked from county to county to see new schools, but unable to see marked regional differences in design. The new universities were encouraged, thanks to the enlightened attitude of the University Grants Committee Architectural Division, to build each according to its own image, and so the UGC's offspring are not 'clones' but diverge and differ within their campus concept.

It could be argued that up-to-date equipment, a fine collection of books and an association of first-rate intellects would create a university, even if housed in a cluster of Nissen huts. Indeed, after World War II, many of the distinguished departments of the colleges of London University were so housed. Common interests and a sense of identity can thrive in a variety of environments. They do not need to be encompassed about in new buildings, nor do new buildings necessarily help. But when there are no buildings at all, and an environment has to be created from scratch, the architect's responsibility is a huge one. The 'miraculous opportunity' offered to him can turn into an expensive experiment with other people's lives. Boris Ford, writing of university planning in 1964 said:

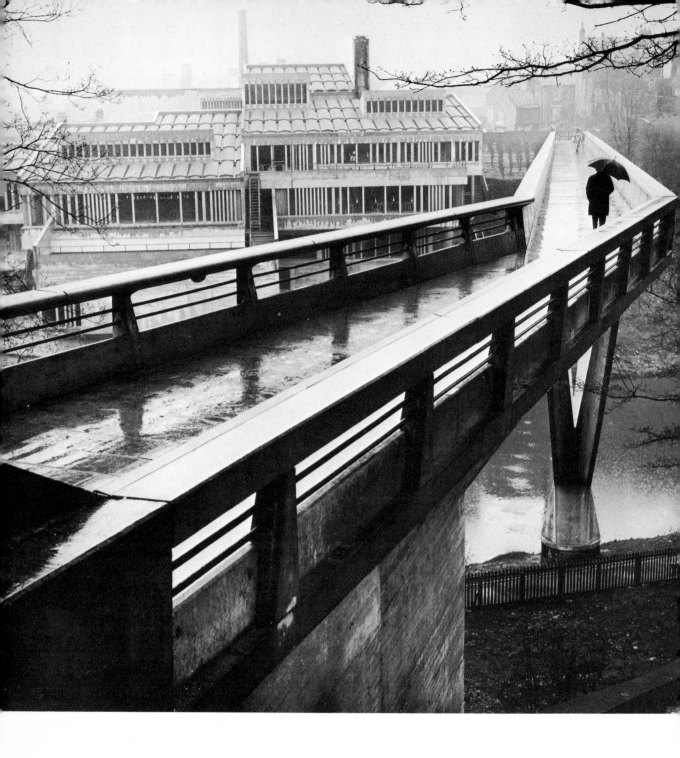

16. Durham is one of Britain's oldest universities, but it contains a fine new university building. Dunelm House, a students' and staff club, was designed by Dick Raines of Architects' Co-Partnership. It is finely tailored to its site on the edge of the River Wear, and its roof lines are in keeping with the ancient city. On the roof are huge concrete 'tiles' up to sixteen feet long, and on the river façade is seen the fenestration pattern which occurs again at Essex University. Dunelm House is linked to the cathedral precinct by the Kingsgate footbridge, designed by Sir Ove Arup.

It seems essential . . . for architects working with academics to remember that whether we plan this social centre or that coffee lounge, or a hall of residence, or whether we arrange for mixed feeding or segregated feeding, this will promote one pattern of student life as against another. We have constantly to be asking ourselves whether the buildings will promote links, whether they will support the academic as well as the intellectual life or encourage private and distant lives.[5]

Each decision about the size of a lecture theatre, the location of a residence block, the colour of curtains, will be tested a thousand times over by generations of students, and as buildings are very expensive, decisions cannot easily be reversed and remade. Students above all other groups of people have a way of expressing their reaction to their environment, if it is unsatisfactory, by re-creating it in their own temporary image: by using a staircase as a place to eat, a landing to hold meetings, or ignoring an available lecture theatre and holding a film show in a bar. At the NUS conference at Lancaster at Easter 1971, students condemned purpose-built residential villages and called for more flats. A single generation of students might show a reversal of this trend, and it is important for architects to remember that students are not a single community and to provide opportunities for change in their plans and their buildings.

As individuals in their university, students will make their first public speech, cast their first vote, work, make love, and all too often become lonely. The glass and concrete environment can be a protective shield, an exhilarating backcloth or even a frightening cell. The charge that the country is building 'architects' universities' underlines the fundamental nervousness about the extent to which academics should contrive their own environment. Those who feel that a university should grow in its own way can point to Oxford and Cambridge. where new colleges like Wolfson and Churchill are built much farther from the university centre than the farthest colleges at, say, Kent but nevertheless rapidly form a well-integrated part of the whole. When the Universities must grow from nothing at the prodigious rate dictated in the 1960s, *someone* has to plan them. and the most important factor is not that the architect should be restrained but that there should be full communication. Sir Hugh Casson in the Bossom Lecture in 1965 said:

> Unless the architect is clear about the academic and social policy of the university for which he is working; if he fails to believe in it, and then to contribute imaginatively to its achievement, then that university will surely find its aim crippled or unfulfilled.[6]

A glimpse of the campuses of the Seven in the 1980s might well show the impact of the phenomenal growth rate in the early years followed by a period of slower growth. The methods and materials, if not the creative thinking, will date them very firmly to the 1960s. At present, part of their difficulties is that they lack a time dimension. It is interesting to compare the Seven with the environment of a not-so-new civic university of about the same scale. Exeter is not a UGC foundation. Founded as a university college attached to London in 1909 (it had been the Royal Albert Memorial College before that), it gained its charter and its independence only in 1955. It is roughly equal in size to members of the Seven, and has a campus site of just over 200 acres on the edge of the town.

17. *A tight triangle of buildings connected by glazed corridors on the campus of Exeter University houses the Chemistry and Physics departments and the Newman building containing six lecture halls. Designed by Sir Basil Spence, the complex was completed in 1968. The corridor in the foreground leads from the Newman building, right, towards the Physics block. Behind is the building for Chemistry research.*

Whilst Sussex had 12,000 applicants for 900 places in 1970, there were over 17,000 for 1,100 places in the same year at Exeter, the only university south-west of Bristol and Bath. In its site in Streatham Park, which includes a steep-sided valley and a magnificent arboretum, it has room to expand and mature, and is preserved from a sense of isolation by its closeness to the city's main railway station. Its architecture extends from the mock-Gothic of the early part of the century to modern buildings by Spence and Holford (plate 17) when a recent expansion turned the college into a campus.

The main residential areas are separated from the teaching buildings by a five-minute walk and are themselves divided into groups, two located in mature bourgeois gardens, interwoven with privately owned houses and public roads. Such a separation on a new campus site would be savagely criticised, as indeed it is at Warwick where physical continuity need not have been broken. At Exeter, however, everyone accepts that the Halls must be several minutes away, for there have always been houses in between, and on the route between Hall and department, students and housewives, campus cars and dairymen's floats are mixed together not artificially but naturally.

In the centre of the main campus and close to the Students' Union is the small Northcott Theatre and a large Concert Hall shared with the city for the monthly visits of the Bournemouth Symphony Orchestra and other less-formal events. A new Sports Hall completes this fairly closely-knit amenity area near the centre, but convenience and architectural unity are low. Exeter has somehow stumbled over the integration of buildings and site. By comparison with the Seven this civic university campus is a mess, but it works and is accepted. No one is to blame for bad building-to-building linkage when some of the buildings have been there longer than anyone's memory, and the ingenious architect who slips a good building into a difficult and half built-up site is praised. In addition, the citizens of Exeter are spared the trauma of suddent contact with students, for they are used to the university being there.

This and most civic universities like it, all with extended facilities in recent years, are relatively harmonious communities, well liked by their members. The Seven, so much publicised, are much more self-critical and altogether less stable. What they badly need is time, and of the very many elements comprising their future this is the one which is most certain of all.

Clearly the interesting question will be whether the new, as they become less new, will fall into line with the Civics and lose their spirit of innovation and excitement. One or two of the students I have met on the campuses have told me that they applied *only* for New Universities, an adventurous and cavalier act when their reputations were still to be made. In consolidating their reputations, it would be a pity if the New University environments ceased to attract the independent of mind.

18. Over the hill from the main site at Exeter are the Birks Halls of Residence.

7 Sussex

One superb building does more to establish the character of Sussex University at Brighton than much of the careful planning on the campuses of the other new universities. The physical impact of this building is great—it overwhelms the visitor, it imprints a visual vocabulary on the long stayer, and it remains in the mind of the Sussex graduate as a key to his student years. The building is Falmer House, social centre of the university, the first building to be built at the first of the Seven. As the student population nears 4,000 in 1971, this building and the university have been in existence for a decade.

The most senior and the largest of the universities, Sussex, under its first Vice-Chancellor Sir John (now Lord) Fulton, was a pioneer in flexible and broad-based courses, and is proud of its capacity for change. It represents a very rapid expansion and also a very rapid assimilation of its environment; it seems established in its 200-acre site in Stanmer Park, whilst other universities, admittedly newer, are still scrambling for a foothold in the landscape. A graduate of Warwick or Lancaster, returning after a gap of two or three years, will find a barely recognisable university confronting him, and will probably look with envy on facilities undreamed of three years before. At Sussex three generations of students—that is batches of students who have worked in the university for three years and departed before the next generation arrived—have entered the university through the same 36 foot high concrete arch, and have seen the campus unfold up the hillside, in the same familiar pink and grey architectural idiom.

In 1959, Sir Basil Spence was invited to submit a plan for a University of Sussex, and the first fifty students were enrolled in 1961. Later that year, the first building was ready for occupation and building has continued without a significant break ever since; by the end of the quinquennial period in 1972 there will be about a million square feet of university at Stanmer Park.

◁ *19. Pink brick and segmental concrete arches are the visual vocabulary of Sussex University. Within the Arts buildings are intimate courtyards which accommodate changes of level up the hillside site.*

49

Whilst the academic structure at Brighton was innovatory and much publicised, the careful inter-relationship between architectural and academic concepts does not exist at Brighton as it does at Essex, for example, or East Anglia. Here, the architect's master plan was a more direct and aesthetic response to the site and landscape, a more random plan. Sir Basil Spence has been quoted as describing its character as 'a kind of frog spawn proliferating in the crevices left between the trees'.[7] If certain aspects of the planning such as pedestrian and vehicular segregation have not been adequately thought through, and if architecture (isolated faculty and social areas) and academic principles (no subject boundaries) are sometimes at odds, Sussex has achieved a 'natural' campus-scape which is relaxed and seems to have been there a long time. The architecture is impressive, without being particularly large. There is a fluent recognition of the emotional potential of buildings and the use of space is sensitive.

The character of the university was affected from the start by the decision to utilise existing accommodation facilities in the town, and to build a largely non-residential university on the Stanmer Park site four miles from the town. The 200 acre site runs from north to south, and has a narrow road frontage. The university occupies a valley and the land climbs fairly steeply upstream to the north. Up the chalky valley sides to the west and east are about twenty distinct buildings or building groups of a fairly constant size, and at least half of them have incorporated the change of level of the terrain into their plan. Between them are open 'courts', landscaped grass terraces, and varied and beautiful trees. Nearly all the buildings are flat-roofed and low, and the building materials are almost exclusively light-coloured concrete and pink fair-faced brick. Sir Basil Spence said, 'a robust and sculptural vocabulary was evolved': the brick and concrete vocabulary is inseparable from a pseudo-vault technique, and rhythmic segmental vaults of different sizes were used in all the early buildings on the campus. They are at the same time monumental, modern and intimate (plate 26), and they are a strong counter-argument to functionalist architecture for they are purely decorative, even misleading as to structure. These weighty-looking concrete vaults are thin hollow 'skins' with cast 'sides' or ends, and are suspended from beams to which they run parallel. In many places these 'vaults' appear to be supported by brick piers, but again this is misleading for the bricks surround concrete dowel posts which take the weight. In several places the pseudo-vaults extend over the edge of the buildings, or as canopies over doorways, as emphatic skylines or projections, but never as functional units. This stylish idiom invented by Sir Basil Spence, Bonnington and Collins, is now too expensive for future buildings, although it can be seen again in London in the same firm's Household Cavalry Barracks, Hyde Park, 1970.

Concrete is a notoriously obtuse material when it comes to weathering and rain-marked concrete surfaces generally have little charm. The concrete pseudo-vault and beam technique as used at Brighton is particularly vulnerable to weathering, for the beams at Falmer House project and are exposed to the rain (plate 21). Perhaps it is the skeletal nature—like a ruin—of Falmer House, or perhaps the historical associations of segmental vaults that makes brown

◁ 20. *Pseudo-vaults triumphantly crown the massive block of the Physics building, one of the first to be built at Sussex. The vaulted undercroft leads to an open courtyard within the buildings.*

21. 'A giant students' climbing frame', with a moat on the inside reflecting the sky and doubling the building's apparent size, Falmer House, the gatehouse courtyard of Sussex University, cost a little over £400,000 to build in 1961, and was awarded the RIBA Bronze Medal in the following year. It has been recognised ever since by successive generations of students at Sussex as a symbol of their environment, as the one building that means Sussex University to them. This is not surprising, for apart from being the first building to go up in Stanmer Park it is also dead in line with the approach footpath from the main road and the railway, and students are drawn through it to the working buildings beyond.

and green algae, and dark wet patches on the concrete acceptable here, when they are disastrous, for example, on the Royal Festival Hall or on the campus at East Anglia. The fact remains that the early buildings at Sussex University have shown weathering in this decade, and they have weathered well.

The visitor arriving by bus or rail will probably use a bare pedestrian subway under the dangerous A27, to emerge on the broad pathway which leads towards the gatehouse quadrangle of Falmer House. The view is reminiscent of an American university campus (though there is a red pillarbox), and this impression is reinforced by the concrete sides to the subway four feet high, announcing UNIVERSITY OF SUSSEX in raised capitals. Whilst most of the new universities signpost themselves for information, Sussex is alone in inscribing its name into its architecture. The high gateway of Falmer House draws the visitor through into the open courtyard, with its internal shallow moat which reflects the walls and doubles the building's apparent size. The aesthetic origins of Falmer House, the architect states, are the Colosseum as it now stands, with its great arches exposed, as well as some of le Corbusier's vaulted houses. Belted around at three levels, and particularly on the top storey, with massive concrete beams, and supported almost all around its square on deep rectangular brick-clad pillars, it is most extravagant of space. More than half of the enclosing framework surrounds a void; much of the top storey is open to the sky. The north end includes a warren of common rooms of different shapes and sizes as well as recreation rooms (billiards and television), a refectory no longer used as such, and a tomb-like debating chamber often used for theatrical rehearsals. Rather more gracious staff common rooms stray round to the south end, especially on the top floor where a wide and pleasant gallery is slung over the old refectory like a ship's bridge, but a bridge so wide that a hundred people can sit in comfortable chairs around scattered low tables. A plan to enclose some of the void areas in the upper storeys may be implemented if the demand for small-sized rooms continues, but any such infilling would mean the loss of the special relationship this building develops with its landscape environment by means of the gaps in the structure. Falmer House, recognised as a major building of its time, was given an RIBA award for outstanding design in 1962.

By 1966, the university had a total of 2,763 students, and Falmer House was bursting at the seams. Some of its functions have since been hived off to other parts of the site, but it still retains a magnetic attraction as a place to meet, to hold meetings, or merely to pass through on the way to other buildings beyond.

Immediately north of Falmer House is the wide open pedestrian space of Fulton Court. To the right are the Science buildings—the early Physics buildings crowned with 'vaults' (plate 20), the circular Chemistry lecture theatre taking advantage of a steep hillside for its raked interior and, farther up the eastern valley side, the Biology and Applied Sciences buildings with their own social rooms and hexagonal lecture hall. Facing these buildings, on the western side of the valley, is the library (plate 22). It is a two-storey building, rectangular in shape, with central 'wells' open to the sky. Phase Three of the building, which doubles the library's size, rides up the hill so that, with roughly the same volume, it looks a storey higher than Phases One and Two. The whole building is based on a 20 foot module, convenient for construction and flexible in use. Open spaces inside are broken up with partitions and bookstacks into

22, 23. *A daunting flight of steps and two massive brick walls— which look like sliding doors— guard the entrance to the library at Sussex. The modern but fortress-like main façade is seen above. Once inside the building (right), everything changes. Reading places are deliberately clustered in small groups to avoid the overwhelming atmosphere of a large hall, and the light-coloured wood and fair-faced brick is welcoming.*

24, 25, 26. The bulging brick building above, the Gardner Centre for the Arts, designed by Sir Basil Spence, Bonnington and Collins, is now a familiar part of the campus at Sussex. It contains a circular theatre (planned by Sean Kenny) with 500 seats and three alternative stages, as well as studios and exhibition areas. Another circular building close by Falmer House is the Meeting House (left), colourfully lit by stained glass in the gaps between its concrete block structure. Right: seminar rooms in Arts 'A' block.

intimate working areas. It offers over a thousand reading places, and has forty-four carrels for postgraduates, meeting the UGC recommendation of one place for four students over all. It has been estimated that the library circulation (the amount of use made of its *lending* facilities) is three times as great as other comparable university libraries, and a computerised lending system now streamlines the issuing of books.

The bulging, curvaceous Gardner Centre for the Arts, to the south of the library, and the Religious Meeting House in the centre of Fulton Court are illustrated in plates 24 and 25. They occupy prominent positions on the campus; and the latter, designed personally by Sir Basil Spence, won a Civic Trust award in 1969. Continuing up the valley, buildings belonging to the Arts area and the Institute of Development Studies lie on the western slopes. The warmth and intimacy of the small courtyards which rise one above the other in the Arts buildings (plate 19) must be a heartening experience for the new arrival, who finds common rooms and small social areas at the end of each corridor within the buildings.

By the time he has reached Arts 'C', the visitor has walked some 300 yards from the underpass, and only now does he confront the first road. To the north of it are the residential areas and the large refectory building. Less happy than the other buildings on the site, the tall refectory block wears its pseudo-vaults like a stiff concrete frill at top floor level and has never quite overcome the resentment which students feel on being prised out of the smaller refectory in Falmer House. Its American-style Scramble Bar is a model of queueless efficiency, and its several bars offer variety of both refreshment and design but the building lacks charm, and the students do not linger in it. Whilst further scientific research buildings and car parks clothe the eastern slopes, two generations of students' residences lie cheek to cheek on the western side. The four quadrangular halls of residence called Park Houses, each housing 120 students, were the first to be built. One—Essex House—has successfully served as a temporary administrative headquarters for its first seven years. In York House, for mixed students, a Henry Moore reclining figure overlooks a courtyard filled with decorative trees. Near to the four halls is the Park Village, the bank-loan financed housing development (plate 28) for students who prefer to live in individual houses in groups of twelve. The

27. *Fulton Court is the name given to the wide grassy area between Falmer House and the crenellated Arts buildings. The entrance, flanked by lecture halls, is by way of the high concrete 'tuning fork', plain by day but impressive when floodlit at night.*

Village was opened in 1969 for 350 students and is now extended to 700. Plans are advanced for a more traditional hall of residence (though linear in design) nearby, which represents a third experiment in student living, and is designed for students who welcome communal life. The rectangular site-plan of Sussex University allows for further development to north, east and west, and there is room for infilling in existing spaces if the need arises.

The architecture is successful partly as a result of the strict observation of certain principles. By keeping all the buildings modest in scale, they are on the whole inviting and welcoming. By respecting the distances between buildings and embracing rather than contradicting the landscape, full value is given to the natural assets of the park. The trees are truly magnificent and are enhanced by the buildings around them. The grassed terraces are invitingly green, and are much used for sitting and sunbathing. The numerous shallow water courses mirror the buildings and reflect the Sussex sky.

The necessity of keeping motor cars and pedestrians apart was recognised at Stanmer Park, as at other university sites, but in underestimating the number of cars the plan displays its greatest weakness. Tarmaced hillside car parks now stretch like grey tarpaulins, spattered with cars, all over the campus, and the trees can no longer cope with the job of hiding them. The central access road through the Science buildings had to be closed as a general thoroughfare for safety reasons, and lies like a paralysed leg across the site, whilst cars wind their way around the back. A peripheral road, planned rather

late in the day, may help to solve the access problem, but the car parks themselves eat up the green and must inevitably approach close to the buildings if they are to be convenient.

Inconvenience in the siting of certain blocks—the refectory building high up the valley, a wet and windy walk from the library or lecture room on a bad day—is the inevitable outcome of the sequential style of planning but the site as a whole, like the original social courtyard of Falmer House, has so many gaps and open spaces that the student at Sussex University never needs to feel confined, or insulated from the road to Brighton and London. To encourage a living campus, and to avoid the dreaded nine-to-five university atmosphere of some red-brick foundations, great efforts were made to provide good facilities, witness the erection of a social building before anything else. The road and rail links with the town of Brighton are excellent, but the realisation of an on-campus community will always result from an intricate combination of factors.

Sussex University has style. So, of course, has Brighton. Unlike some of the more modest civic communities, like Colchester (population 75,000), which have come to harbour new universities, Brighton has always had a glamour as well as a population (250,000 with Hove) into which a student community could merge as readily as at such red-brick universities as Nottingham. A very attractive town will inevitably work against the vice-chancellor's desire to see the university in action seven days a week, and Brighton is only a quick sixty-minute train ride away from London. The country villages are attractive too, and one cannot blame academic staff at Sussex for being drawn by the special attractions of the Wealden countryside and wanting to live in it.

28. Park Village consists of 'streets' of terraced houses in which live more than half of the students resident on the campus. Windows either overlook the park, as above, or face each other across the narrow pedestrian streets.

Sussex, therefore, suffers by being in an attractive place and, despite its amenities, students and staff flee the campus now as in the early days, especially at the weekends. Visiting students from neighbouring colleges, attending perhaps a single sports function or a union meeting, look with envy at the facilities of this university and its superb physical environment, and wonder why, on a mid-term Sunday, the place is deserted. This may change as the proportion of students living on the site rises. Pressure for lodgings from a student population nearing 10,000 (if one includes the local Polytechnic and College of Education) has caused the council, which once wooed the university with its welcoming landladies, to turn about and urge the authorities to house 40 per cent of its students on the campus. This will mean 1,500 in 1971 and proportionately more when the university approaches 6,000 in 1976.

There was a marvellous pioneering spirit about the campus in the early days, as original members of staff and students recall. This feeling is not exclusive to Sussex, of course, but the architecture gave a sense of exhilaration which matched the mood, and sustained those who found it hard to believe that a university which was not an old university could have any atmosphere at all. In the building of something entirely new at Brighton, full credit must be given to Sir Basil Spence, whose architectural presence is so continuously felt.

After the first few years, the initial time advantage of the Sussex campus disappeared and when exciting plans got under way at East Anglia, Essex and elsewhere, it ceased to be the place which immediately sprang to mind at the very mention of new universities. But the environment it had created—it was the first to make the American word 'campus' acceptable in England— has certainly not been eclipsed by later developments, and many feel it has not been equalled.

8 York

'We in the north have been looked upon as a rude and barbarous people, and a university would be a special means of washing from us the stain of rudeness and incivility,' argued the petition for a University of York in 1641,[8] but without success. In 1947 York again made representations for a university, this time to the University Grants Committee, only to be refused once more, as academic hostility to new foundations had not given way to the later expansionist thinking. It was therefore in 1959—the time of establishment of the University of Sussex—that the local promotion board, headed by the Archbishop of York, tried again, and this time York got UGC approval on the same day as East Anglia, in April 1960, to become equal second of the seven new universities.

The appointment in 1961 of Lord James as Vice-Chancellor, and Robert Mathew, Johnson-Marshall and Partners as consultant architects, began what Lord James has described as a totally educative process in detailed university planning. A continual dialogue with the architects resulted in the Development Plan of 1962,[9] providing for the first 3,000 students in ten years of growth. This detailed plan was the first of its kind for a new foundation, and is a particularly valuable document today for comparative purposes. It would have been carried through almost without modification if the flow of finance had been as anticipated.

The Heslington site, of 190 acres including the nineteenth-century Heslington Hall, and one and a half miles outside York but encroaching upon the village of Heslington, was the planner's raw material. Although the only new university site to abut on to a village, it contained little building and with the adjacent common land known as Walmgate Stray represented a wedge of green landscape approaching more nearly to the heart of its mother city than do any of the other new campuses. The land was mainly low-lying and marshy, and crossed by the winding Heslington Road. At the northern end the site rises to a ridge which is dominated by the fortress-like tower of the York Water Board.

The vice-chancellor opted for a college system to give the members of the university a focus for loyalty and identification as the university grew, and thus the first major planning decision was taken: there would be several social nuclei on the site. Apart from the Science Studies, requiring special laboratory facilities, the physical location of the work-centres for such subjects as History, Economics and Sociology were to be within the colleges, so that 'faculty' buildings could be avoided. The pattern of teaching, heavily weighted towards tutorials with a maximum of four students, was then invoked to determine the kind of space required for learning. A high percentage of on-campus residence—50 per cent to 66 per cent—was a third early determinant in the plan. The problem of residence at York University has always been regarded as a key factor in its development, and in the Development Plan emphasis was laid on the need for both student and staff accommodation on the site. While providing a tutorial room for each member of staff within the colleges, it was hoped to build housing for a third of the teaching staff on the site in a close relationship with the colleges.

The figure of 300 undergraduates was originally chosen by the planners as an optimum size for colleges 'small enough for their members to be known to each other', and following the 50 per cent residential principle, 150 study-bedrooms would be required from the start. With a target of 2,500 undergraduates in the first ten years, eight such colleges were envisaged, and allocated positions on the ground plan. Similarly, the science departments, the library and the Central Hall were given sites, and a circulatory system for pedestrians was organised which would allow no obstacles and which would carry straight through some of the densest areas within the campus.

The physical nature of the site was slightly intractable, and the creation of a permanent fifteen-acre lake was suggested both to drain the area and to provide a focal point for the buildings. Water, however often it is bridged, divides rather than unites, and the dispersed plan which results consists of nodes linked stellar-fashion by a network of covered pathways, and obstructed by the lake itself and the re-aligned Heslington Road, renamed 'University Road', which was planned to be part of a segregated vehicle-access system. This high-speed road carries more traffic than anticipated and provides a certain amount of noise and danger, although it does remove the sense of isolation which may occur when a university is built at the end of a cul-de-sac, as occurs at Lancaster and Essex.

The planners were concerned from the start to provide a 'memorable' environment for students and staff. 'It is necessary to try to discover the characteristic forms and relationships of the buildings in their setting which correspond to the academic and social ideals of the university on the one hand, and to the social and geographical context of the York district on the other',

29. Students walk along one of the covered ways in Derwent College, while ▷
fountains play at the edge of the artificial lake.

Overleaf: 30. Derwent College from the south. The horizontal top of the CLASP
buildings is varied with fibreglass turrets over the dining hall and monoclinal outcrops over the library, but the outstanding features on the northern skyline are the concrete mushroom shape of the Chemistry department's water tower, and the sculptural boilerhouse chimney. It is a pity they are so close together.

31. *The entrance to Derwent College has an informal atmosphere, with small changes of level successfully breaking down the open spaces.*

says the report—a much more business-like approach to the environment, one might say, than at Sussex. Academic staff, especially senior scientists, were appointed as early as possible so they would be able to influence the design of their specialised buildings.

The medieval King's Manor within the city of York and the rather dilapidated Heslington Hall itself were put for restoration and conversion into the hands of Bernard Feilden, and they provided teaching and administrative centres whilst the main site was getting on its feet. In order to give a sense of completeness at each stage, and to reduce the annoyance and noise of building works in progress, the phasing of development was planned to radiate not in concentric circles but in four broad arcs westward of Heslington Hall. This phasing has been most successfully achieved, and was made possible by the completion of the site works—the draining of the land, the creation of the lake and the realignment of the road—at an early stage. Fairly small compact buildings, regularly spaced, would increase in number on a widening front as the plan proceeded westwards.

A most significant factor affecting the visual environment of York University was the decision to employ a modified version of the CLASP system of building for all but the most specialised buildings. A temporary shortage of bricks and local wet-trade builders were among the reasons for this decision, but the main consideration was speed of construction, for CLASP is a dry technique consisting of a steel frame with wooden floors and external light concrete cladding. Thus a significant aid to the rapid growth of the university in the early 1960s will leave its visual imprint on the environment for ever. The CLASP system undoubtedly gives an impression of impermanence, especially from the outside, although the large standard-size cladding panels allow a greater variety in façades than might be supposed. The material responds to light and weather less than other concrete surfaces; it is remarkably resistant to staining, but only brightens up slightly in sunlight. The aggregate was carefully chosen to match local gravels and to harmonise with the landscape. It is sad that an aggregate containing marble chips, which would have sparkled in sunlight, had to be rejected on grounds of cost.

The CLASP buildings which comprise the colleges are grouped with great invention, but one disadvantage of the system is the lack of flexibility it allows for varying roof-lines, and unfortunately those buildings such as the Physics block, which for practical reasons did not use CLASP, have failed to rise to the challenge of giving the university a really distinguished skyline. In fact, it remains for the brick chimneys and roofs of Heslington Hall to provide the most interesting backing to the uniform low grey buildings of the colleges.

Derwent and Langwith, the first two colleges to be built, are very similar in design, as in the other collegiate universities, Kent and Lancaster, and in fact are so close to each other, and connected by a covered way, that it is difficult to be sure where one ends and the other begins. Each has an open social area at the entrance, and a dining hall, snack bar, exhibition concourse, and library at the 'core' of the college. The prospectus states that in these colleges 'the university architects had one particular aim . . . to create a group of rooms where social contact at all levels would be easy to achieve but also, if desired, equally easy to avoid'. The architects were aware of a hostility to the traditional Oxbridge college image and the possible control over student activities which the communal life implies. Around the edge of the colleges blocks of

32, 33. At the heart of the campus, the Central Hall, designed by John Speight, contrasts with other buildings. In the underbelly of the tiered auditorium is a large bar, with fine views of the lake.

study-bedrooms for students of the same sex project as wings, and approach close to the eastern extremity of the lake (plate 4).

To the west, two more colleges constructed in CLASP, Vanbrugh and Goodricke, are built one on each side of the lake, whilst a fifth and larger college, Alcuin, lies on the higher land to the north of University Road. Also north of the road is the site for Wentworth College, to be begun in 1972, and between them is the Morrell library. Least successful both architecturally and functionally of the libraries of the Seven, it was located for visual reasons on its high site at a corner of the university rather than centrally, and will expand in due course north-eastwards to provide facilities for 2,000 readers and 750,000 volumes. Although lying within the pedestrian circuit, the library can only be approached under cover from one college, Alcuin, and it is much exposed to wind and to noise from the road. For functional reasons, the CLASP technique was not used for this building, nor for the Central Hall and the Physics building which face each other across the lake.

The Central Hall, capacity 1,200, is cantilevered out over the lake (plates 32 and 33), and its roof is suspended by means of two stays anchored to a concrete support at the rear. A gallery runs round the building at a high level, and the pattern of staircases on the rear elevation helps to relieve the rather pudding-like shape of the whole. It is very well appointed internally, and seats fold back to make an examination hall for two hundred. It is chiefly used for speech functions, whilst the smaller Lyons Concert Hall (plate 34) is used for music and also houses the Music Department.

To avoid a closely-knit and perhaps rather daunting 'science area' the three major science disciplines are rather inconveniently separated from one another, and lie at eastern, southern and western extremities of the site, each with a large car park close by. Car parks also fringe the side of the road, with space for over 2,000 cars by 1971, yet the presence of cars is less obtrusive at York than at other campuses, perhaps because of the flatness of the site and the making of seven separate vehicle entrances (as against one at East Anglia). Phalanxes of small and rather temporary-looking private residences for academic staff infiltrate the spaces in the site, including the modest house of the vice-chancellor, and a computer building and language centre have been built at the heart of the site.

Orientation is not easy within the university, as one is not aware of the radiating nature of the plan when on the ground. The lake, which has a festive

34. *The Lyons Concert Hall, with seats for 450.*

35. *Vanbrugh College library and reading room overlooks the lake with its water-spout. The bulky and unglamorous Physics buildings lie beyond.*

air with boats in summer and always looks slightly Japanese because of its covered bridges and weeping willows, crosses the geographical centre of the plan, and the Central Hall is supposed to be the node from which a five-minute walk will take anyone to the periphery. In fact, the centre of gravity of the university seems closer to the eastern end, where the early colleges are joined to Heslington Hall and the concentration of activity is greatest. The extensive pedestrian routeway starts at Heslington Hall and is roughly circular, with loops and tongues to outlying parts of the site. In all, eight bridges and some stepping stones are necessary to connect the various parts of the university across the lake and the road. The route is shown, dotted, on the plan on page 61.

The cutback in finance has caused the building programme to fall short of the Development Plan by two colleges, and the governmental pressure for higher student numbers is having a significant effect on the principles of planning, for the colleges originally intended for 300 students have to be stretched to 450 to meet the expected figure of 2,700 by the end of 1972. The prospect of new residential non-collegiate buildings on the campus might have to be faced if loan-financed schemes are called upon, and in view of the lodgings

36. *The ramp and steps in the picture above are part of the pedestrian route leading to the Morrell library and crossing the busy University Road.*

problems in York, where 1,000 units is a maximum figure, provision has to be made to house 1,700 students by 1972, an increase of 500 over the figure for 1970. At the same time, changes in building costs, especially the cost of steel, make CLASP a less attractive proposition and the most recent additions to Vanbrugh College have a concrete block skeleton and CLASP cladding only to preserve external unity. The need to provide a sixth college within a strict budget may mean an abandonment of concrete in favour of wood cladding, although this need not result in a lowering of aesthetic standards.

In the landscape, the artificial lake is a dominating factor, but tree planting and, in particular, the renewal of the formal gardens of Heslington Hall contribute to a gracious and attractive environment for the buildings, and the impression of over-tight planning or paternalism is resisted.

Andrew Derbyshire was the partner most directly concerned with the planning of York University from the beginning, and Robert Mathew, Johnson-Marshall and Partners, also acting as consultants for both Bath University and Stirling University, must now be regarded as the firm most experienced in new university design.

9 East Anglia

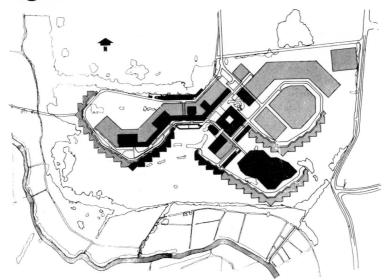

Lord Clark chose to conclude his television series 'Civilisation' in front of the residential terraces at the University of East Anglia, a stage set or perhaps a backdrop for the pursuit of learning in the present and the future. Of the Seven, he chose the one whose architecture has most consciously created a visual impression of experiment and enquiry, yet without the use of bizarre forms or materials, and notably without recourse to any academic architectural precedent.

'I want to work,' said a young lecturer from Germany, 'in buildings which look as though something interesting is going on inside,' and he likes working at the University of East Anglia.

Commissioned as consultant architect in April 1962, Denys Lasdun produced this first 'urban' scheme amongst the Seven for a compact dense development, soon followed by Essex, Lancaster, and Warwick. The plans aimed to integrate buildings and landscape with a total vision, and to interpret the client's requirements visually as well as functionally.

The site consisted of 165 acres of parkland, partly used as a golf course, two miles outside Norwich and fringing the River Yare. Lasdun was delighted by it, and viewed it in all weathers, on foot and from a helicopter. He described the site as '. . . itself an organism: water, marsh, slope, trees, meadow, parkland, set in East Anglian landscape'.[10] He was determined to retain these characteristics and to make the most of another feature: the view from the site across the river to more open land. The university has since bought a further 100 acres on the far bank of the river, and therefore now controls the future usage of the land on all sides.

The Development Plan appeared in December 1962. In addition to the guiding principles of compactness, a five-minute walking radius and pedestrian

◁　*37.　The Suffolk and Norfolk Terraces face the river and expose their backs, like stage scenery, to the service road and the flanking teaching wall. The elevated walkway, with solid concrete balustrade, is also an overhead service duct. It allows access at second floor level as well as from the ground where the cars are parked.*

73

and vehicle segregation (all of which were fast becoming *de rigueur* in campus plans), it was greatly influenced by major decisions of academic planning, interpreted to the architects by the Vice-Chancellor, Frank Thistlethwaite. The university was to be unitary, dominated by seven or eight broadly-based schools of study which would provide both academic and social focuses. A close physical relationship in the architecture would help to blur the edges between disciplines and to avoid the hard and fast boundaries which are implied by isolated 'faculty' blocks. At the same time, recognising the vice-chancellor's view that 'the [academic] growing points have recently tended to be at the interstices between established disciplines', the teaching buildings would need a flexibility to accommodate unforeseen needs.

High priority was to be given to the library as a central feature which should be attractive to students, and social facilities for all members of the university should be made available in a 'University House'. Student residence was to be developed from a 'modulus' of not more than twelve students sharing facilities in the manner of an Oxbridge 'staircase', and the planners tried also to bear in mind the contemporary student's dislike of enforced formality and his demand for greater independence to live as he wishes.

The result of this brief was a linear plan in which a continuous wall of teaching buildings faced a chain of student residences across a narrow access route, in which pedestrians were elevated above ground level on a walkway, and vehicles provided with some parking space alongside the road below. The whole double-chain was wrapped like a pair of wiggly chromosomes around a sanctuary area or 'harbour' containing the central library, as can be seen on the plan, page 73.

As a module for a complete university, this is the most romantic and intellectually appealing of the Seven. In practice it has proved less than satisfactory on several scores, most of which are associated with building delays, the cutback in finance and an unsatisfactory system of building priorities. The key, however, to the shortcomings of the university at a half-way stage is not in the over-planning of the total environment, but in the planning of an over-large university. The brief was for a university of 3,000 and the plan was for double that number over a period of fifteen years, with growth projections

38. The heart of the University Plain was not the first part to be built. The model below shows University House, centre, with shops and refectory alongside, between the library (left) and the sports hall (right) as they should appear in 1972.

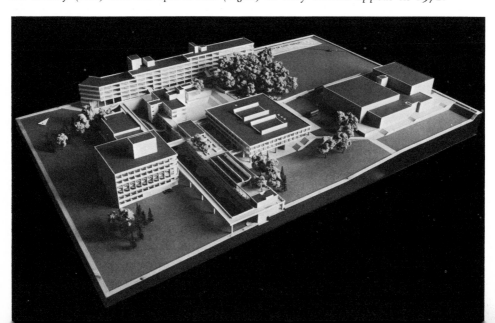

39. *The University Village, designed by Bernard Feilden. The temporary refectory is on the left, and in the centre is the permanent home of the university's art collection and the School of Fine Arts and Music.*

to 10,000 and 15,000. The expansionist mood of the time justified this ambitious scheme, which was followed by even bigger ones at Essex and Warwick in their Development Plans—where the shortfall has been equally great—but if the Lasdun plan had been for 3,000 students it would have had a good chance of completion within a single decade. As it is, it will never be judged in full, for like a dinosaur expiring with the disappearance of its staple diet, it is becoming fossilised through lack of adequate finance, and only a few central vertebrae and ribs lie on the ground (shown in black in the plan), giving little idea of its full extent and shape.

The architect was asked to provide a 'sense of place' and to make sure that the university was a 'coherent entity at each stage of growth so that early generations of students should not have the sense of living in a broken and unfinished development'. He replied, 'What we shall build in East Anglia is an organism which is complete *and* incomplete, which can grow and change, but which does not produce a wilderness of mechanisms'.[11]

Great imagination and concentration on detail have ensured that the Lasdun buildings give the university its 'sense of place', but by 1968 several buildings had got behind schedule and it was clear that time and finances would not allow the plan to be completed. Denys Lasdun gave up the architectural consultancy and Bernard Feilden, associated with the planning from 1962, succeeded him. Buildings of a different character are therefore now beginning to appear on the site, and the car parking, circulation system and central area are reorganised. The model shown in plate 38 gives an indication of how the heart of the university should appear in 1972.

Despite the 'urban' master plan, various factors in the early history of the UEA affected its growth and kept it dispersed.

The 165 acre golf course contained no buildings usable as temporary accommodation but was adjacent to Earlham Park, and the seventeenth-century Earlham Hall, home of Elizabeth Fry, was taken over as an administrative centre in 1962. Whilst it was clear that permanent buildings on the main site or 'University Plain' could not be ready at least until 1965, a surprise gift of twelve acres across the Earlham Road made it possible to open the university to students in October 1963, by the building of a temporary 'university village' there. The architect was Bernard Feilden, and 137,000 square feet of teaching, social and library space were built at a cost of £500,000. No residential accommodation was made here, but the Horsham airfield barracks, four miles away, were commandeered to provide a living environment for all first-year students—which of course meant *all* students in the first university year.

Both the village and the former air base continue as important parts of the university, and are no longer regarded as temporary. The village (plate 39) was so successful in creating a good environment that students in 1965 would walk over to the main site and wonder how the incoherent disorder of concrete and mud and cranes could ever replace it as a living centre for the university. As the main site grew more comprehensible and more popular, the village gained a further fillip when a huge traditional barn on its own river frontage was converted into a students' dance hall and boathouse, and the nineteenth-century Earlham Lodge became available as a dignified social centre for members of the staff.

The visitor approaching the university along Earlham Road finds arrows pointing in opposite ways directing him to the University Plain, housing the main schools of study and roughly half the students, and the University Village half a mile distant, housing the School of Fine Arts and the newly-introduced schools of study whilst at an infant stage. A third arrow points to Earlham Hall. There should really be two more; one pointing four miles north to the Horsham Barracks, the other back into the city of Norwich where a further 500 students live in digs.

A new but one-way route leads into the main site from Earlham Road, and the massive buildings of the Lasdun plan are approached from the rear. Both the teaching wall and the residential terraces curl round to face the river, and in the sea of cars (sadly underestimated in the original scheme) parked near the entrance road, one has a strong impression of being backstage. The huge teaching wall, five and six storeys high, is not quite joined up and affords glimpses of the backs of the residences, where Lasdun himself anticipated the 'backyard mess of undergraduates activities, games rooms, laundries, cars and bicycles'. It is not, indeed, a pretty sight, but prettiness was never the architect's intention; he was concerned with a counterpoint between the open landscape to the south and the buildings on the slopes which face it. If the university is approached from the river side by the footpath from Bluebell Road to the south-east, the impression is quite different. Again the heavily-glazed tall teaching wall dominates, flat-topped but capped by massive sculptural concrete blocks containing lift machinery, water tanks, etc., and giving an alert and varied skyline. In front of it are ranked the famous ziggurat residential terraces (plate 41) in a jagged apron, subtly varied in plan so that the massing of the buildings changes as the visitor approaches. Without using any shapes other than conventional rectangles, the ziggurats convey the impression of a futuristic town. Very fully glazed, the façade is a marvellous blaze of light at night.

40.   *The uncompromising façade of the teaching wall, right.*   ▷

41.Overleaf: *'Great ships floating on a sea of green.' The Lasdun terraces overlook the lawns in front of the River Yare. Interviewed on Thames Television, the architect said 'I just call it a harbour because it's the biggest space in the university, and in a sense it's the monument of the university, instead of a building being the monument'.*

42. *A long, straight flight of stairs leads down from the walkway into the Lasdun terraces, where all the rooms face the river.*

The architect adapted the vice-chancellor's modulus of twelve-student units with shared services into stepped pyramids each housing sixty students in 'layers' of twelve. Taking advantage of the rising land, the residences are set back into the hill, and each storey interlocks into the one below so that seven levels can be accommodated within a rise of fifty feet. All student rooms face the river, looking south-east or south-west, and the saw-edged plan gives a view to the maximum number, just as it gave visibility to archers in medieval fortifications. The stepped section allows each room to have a terrace (plate 6) and a split ceiling height—8 feet 6 inches at the front and 6 feet 10 inches at the rear. Apart from bathrooms and services, the ziggurats are only one room thick, and at the back there is an undercroft for car parking, the upper floors being propped up on concrete stilts. The lower two floors are below road level, and the top two are about the level of the overhead walkway, but as access is available from both these points there is no need for lifts. Instead, a single flight of stairs runs down to the foot of each block from the walkway at the rear, rather like a companionway on a liner, an effect which is enhanced by the fittings and the decoration (plate 42).

The rear of the terraces, windowless and drab with large pre-cast panels, gives little hint of comfort (plate 37). Pairs of cubic concrete projections at the very top give an air of constant alertness from the river side, but battleship menace from the rear. Disappearing down the companionway from the walkway brings one suddenly into an unexpected world of comfort and warmth, with rich fitted carpets, plate-glass mirrors and handsome student rooms. These are fitted with furniture in creosoted wood and bamboo roller blinds which are excellent as sunblinds but transparent as 'curtains'. There are some double rooms and a tutor's flat in each block, and each floor has a kitchen at the 'point' of the plan. Optimistically called a 'breakfast room'—the meal least likely to be eaten in it—it is sparsely furnished with equipment, and students queue at midday and in the evenings to use its meagre facilities. Here, as elsewhere amongst the Seven, the increase in self-catering by students has taken the planners by surprise, and the kitchens are slowly being equipped with cookers and refrigerators.

The terraces are well liked and the modulus of twelve grouped in blocks of sixty is socially acceptable. The intricacy of the architecture prevents the groups from feeling isolated, and six hundred students are housed in ten of these blocks arranged as two terraces on either side of the 'harbour' area. The long-term Lasdun plan provided for nearly fifty, but as the cost per student at the time of building was £1,300 and the appeal fund which financed them is almost exhausted, it is unlikely that these striking buildings will be seen to spread round the corners of the site, as shown on the master plan.

Between the two terraces is the six-storey library, a relaxed and beautifully furnished building of modular construction, with broad fins around its perimeter and entrance at the third storey level (plate 43). The reason for this high entrance is that the approach to the library—as to the suite of four lecture rooms alongside, also by Lasdun—is by the elevated walkway that maintains

43. *When the handsome library is complete, its size will be almost doubled. The blank wall on the right will be the attachment point for 'stage two', which will continue the pattern of the façade.*

44. It rains, on the average, on more than 200 days every year at the university of East Anglia, and though the overhead walkway separates students from cars, there is no protection from the weather. The cast concrete and the concrete blocks shine brightly when the sun is out, but the surfaces look miserable when they are wet.

constant level against the slope of the land, starting at ground level on the higher land at the eastern end of the teaching wall.

The teaching wall itself varies in height from five to six storeys, although a constant ceiling height is maintained within the buildings, and the pattern of fenestration is strong (plate 40). The high ceilings (9 feet 6 inches) of the science buildings with their heavy service requirements are therefore passed on to the arts buildings, where cubic capacity on this scale is wasteful.

Many people feel that the concept of interpenetration of disciplines by means of architectural union is unattainable and almost as soon as the Chemistry School had moved in, it was decided to fit heavy doors to prevent students from the School of English and American Studies from straying into it. Now they are kept locked. The structure of the teaching wall does not provide a flexible environment which adapts according to needs, but rather an office-building type of environment into which the different disciplines must be persuaded to fit, willy nilly. The link building now being completed will join the Biology School through Mathematics, Physics, Environmental Studies, Chemistry, English, American, European, Economics and Social Studies in a continuous dog-leg, although the high costs of its special construction and the UGC application of norms for future buildings means that the wall, like the ziggurat terraces, has gone as far as it will go.

The final stage of development in the quinquennium ending in 1972 is concentrated at the eastern end of the site, in an urgent effort to provide some of the facilities which the main site has so far had to do without. Under the new consultant architect, Bernard Feilden, a refectory block has been built close to the library, and a computer centre near the lecture block. A very popular but dull-looking sports hall designed by Birkin Haward was opened in 1971, and nearby is the site for the university union building, shops, a bus station and chaplaincy. Farther to the east, on high ground, is the second residential development, Waveney Terrace, designed by the Norwich Partnership to house 750 students when complete (plate 7).

If the Lasdun terraces are the university's Mary, then here is its Martha. Designed to the low-cost limits imposed by loan-financed schemes, the block could hardly be barer. It has minimum maintenance, with no painted surfaces, and minimal furniture. Staircases are basic to the point of being dangerous and temporary expedients such as planks are used to make them safer. Whilst I would not wish to criticise the architects for failing to produce better-appointed buildings at extremely low cost, to congratulate all concerned on having achieved the buildings for this low figure suggests that the terraces are an adequate living environment. They are certainly not equal to the rest.

Eastward development stops at present at this point, not far from the exit to Bluebell Road. At the western end, and across the river, site works are proceeding in preparation for later developments and here are the playing fields, the sports pavilion and also the privately financed research institutes, cautiously being encouraged to be built near the university for mutual benefit.

The University of East Anglia, with an East Anglian motto, 'do different', has made an impressive start as an academic institution with an appetite for innovation. It introduced credit for term-time work as well as examination results with its degree assessment, and invoked what the vice-chancellor describes as 'a grouping of cognate disciplines' to counteract over-specialisation. The students have shown themselves, as in most of the Seven, forceful and dynamic in response to the university around them. But the environment at East Anglia, imaginatively and lovingly planned, dignified by striking buildings as part of a single-minded vision of what the university ought to look like, stands in danger of losing all visual coherence as plans, each with merits, are overlaid one on top of another. Denys Lasdun has said, of architects in general, '. . . our job is to give the client, on time and on cost, *not* what he wants, but what he never dreamed he wanted, and when he gets it he recognises it as something he wanted all the time'.[12]

Lasdun went part of the way towards building this dream until rising costs put its realisation out of reach. Buildings were delayed and postponed, and the concept began to crack. For the university site to have to exist for five years without a restaurant, without a bank and without shops is absurd, and the more pragmatic approach of the present will make the UEA a more functional campus, even if it is prose replacing the poetry.

10 Kent

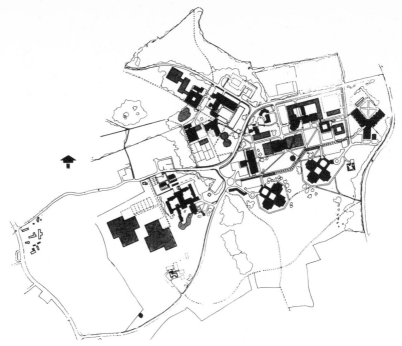

'We have to think of the future, but we are very conscious of the fact that it is not necessarily our future,' said Dr Templeman, Vice-Chancellor of the University of Kent, to the Seminar on University Planning in 1964.[13] He believed that the expansionist thinking of the 1960s was misleading architects and planners into designing finite schemes which would never be realised because of altered circumstances along the way. The master plan for a new university was not for Kent.

Two local factors had a considerable influence at the early stage. Firstly, the site itself, nearly 300 acres of farmland on the crown of a hill overlooking Canterbury, contained no large building which could be converted for university use (such as Heslington Hall at York) to solve the problem of accommodating the university at its infant stage. Secondly, the prominence of the site in relation to an amenity-conscious small town containing a noble cathedral meant that tall buildings which might rival the cathedral for attention, or temporary buildings of makeshift appearance, would have been unpopular with, if not forbidden by, the local authorities who had generously given the site, and would have been a poor start to town-gown relations. In addition, the conviction shared by Dr Templeman and Lord Holford, who was appointed as consultant architect in 1962, that temporary buildings tend to stay around for much longer than planned and to become permanent until they fall apart, increased the urgency for permanent buildings.

The short period of time between the arrival of the vice-chancellor in spring 1963 and the arrival of nearly 500 students in autumn 1965 gave Kent a reputation for breakneck speed, whilst at the same time turning its face firmly from the idea of a master plan on the site. This seems a formula for disaster at every level, from the provision of drains and services in inconvenient places, to the lack of thought for social needs in an out-of-town campus. In practice, the open-ended nature of the concept led to very positive if rapid thinking

◁ *45.   The great dining hall at Rutherford College. Through the window is a view of Canterbury Cathedral, and at the U-shaped table the staff dine.*

about the buildings which were immediately required, and the change in the flow of finance since the expansive days of 1963 and 1964 has already proved the value of the vice-chancellor's caution in attaching his university too firmly to plans which might never be realised. 'None of us knows the dimensions of the national situation. None of us would care to say what academic opportunities lie ahead,' he said.

The principal consideration was the concept of rapid growth common to all the Seven. A collegiate system was chosen and the need to provide a 'complete' university at each stage was stressed so as to give the student a sense of permanence. It was felt that a college should provide a total environment and that the rapid growth in numbers could be phased to coincide with the completion of new colleges. The university would have one container, then two, then three, etc. An essential difference between this scheme and the similar one at Lancaster is that Kent does not have a 'spine', and the buildings, instead of being a continuous proliferation like leaf buds on a stem, are physically distinct and scattered across the site, so that when the jump into the new college comes, it is more noticeable.

The physical character of the buildings as they have turned out suggests that the consultant architect, although rejecting the master plan, wanted to create an 'atmosphere' and that his attitude was a romantic one. The commanding position of the hilltop overlooking Canterbury, now covered with the weighty masonry blocks of the university, suggests a fortified town like its mother city, or a castle like nearby Dover—an impression which would have been even stronger if a plan to build linking walls between buildings had been implemented.

In fact, Lord Holford's attempts to create a centre of gravity in the university at the top of the hill was adversely affected by the uncertainty of the campus boundaries, only resolved finally in 1970 when the southern borders between the university and the town were rescheduled from university sports ground to private housing, and the university was given a comparable area of land for sports fields on the far border of the site to the north. The idea envisaged by Lord Holford of building an S-shaped line of colleges, like stars in the Great Bear, bending downhill towards Canterbury, is frustrated by these changes in the boundaries.

When there were five major buildings on the campus in 1966 Lord Holford resigned and his place as consultant architect was taken by William Henderson of Farmer and Dark, who was engaged at the time in designing one of the colleges. Since 1966 there has been some filling in of the spaces between the buildings. As yet barely perceptible, the intention of William Henderson to insert buildings into existing spaces, creating surprise views and interrupting the broad vistas of grass and glass, will alter the character as development continues, especially as finance for large buildings is unlikely within the next decade. Thus Kent shares with East Anglia and Warwick the prospect of an about-turn in environment resulting from a change of consultant architect.

The university now recognises four clearly defined areas on its site, two on each side of Giles Lane, a public road which crosses it. First, the open parkland slopes with the massive masonry colleges at the top and, second, the 'central' area on the hilltop itself, densely used and more urban in character. Both lie to the south of the road and are visible from the city. To the north is the Sciences area, surrounded by carefully protected but rather scrubby woodland,

46. *The geometry of Rutherford College is broken down into small units for the common rooms. The intimate design here, with an octagonal open courtyard, is an improvement on the vast impersonal common room at Eliot College.*

and beyond it the open area for playing fields. The road itself is not heavily used by through traffic and is, of course, incorporated into the circulation scheme for university vehicles. Along the road, however, are some private properties which penetrate into the university site and prevent any radical reorganisation of the western end of the central area whilst they are in private ownership. The main site was compulsorily purchased farmland, but the local and county authorities were not prepared to uproot families in large numbers by extending compulsory purchase to private residences. However, it is the university's intention to buy the houses if possible when they come onto the market. The farmland site is a very open one, and although it has a splendid view over the city, it has few local landscape advantages, and in particular lacks the mature and varied trees which add so much grace to the campus at Sussex, and would have given some protection against the prevailing wind. Tree planting is now actively under way, particularly on the slopes which face the city, but these plans will naturally take time to show any benefits. The site works at Kent had to include the making of a new road from the central area towards the city, to relieve the pressure on Giles Lane, and this is now being supplemented with a second road leading to the northern end of the site through the playing fields.

Apart from the special-purpose buildings for Science Studies, academic head-quarters as well as all teaching facilities were originally housed in the colleges, and any analysis of the university made up to 1968 would rest heavily on a study of Eliot College, the first encapsulated community designed by Lord Holford and Partners. This was opened in 1965, and its twin brother Rutherford came a year later. No major modification was possible as there was very little time between the building of the first and the second, and they may as well be regarded as simultaneous. The more recent colleges differ widely in conception and the first two colleges now have a less overwhelming effect on the university as a whole, but their characteristic symmetrical plan is still taken as a symbol for the university. It consists of a stubby Greek cross with broad arms and a hollow centre. The arms themselves are squares, with student and tutorial teaching rooms on all exterior walls, the central areas being occupied by administration, lecture rooms, dining hall and common rooms respectively. The conception has the appeal of a mathematical problem and the complexity of its realisation is one of its disadvantages. The colleges are shown in plates 45–48 and their architectural features described there in more detail.

Most of the early arrivals at Canterbury were grateful for the delineation which the first colleges gave, but the aesthetic shortcomings—for the design is much criticised for being bunker-like, inscrutable, and for its rooftop excrescences—are the price that Kent has had to pay, just like the choice of CLASP at York, for doing things in a great rush. Claustrophobic is the word most frequently tossed about in relation to Eliot and Rutherford Colleges, partly as a result of the lack of natural lighting in the main corridors and some of the teaching rooms, and partly the traditional formality of College living which is built into these very inflexible buildings.

Contracts for the third and fourth colleges were given, consistent with the original policy of employing several architects for buildings on the campus, to Farmer and Dark, and Williamson, Faulkner Brown. The third, Keynes, by Farmer and Dark, is an organic grouping around central facilities without symmetry, and the fourth college, Darwin, by Faulkner Brown, has a starkly

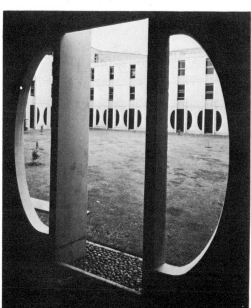

47, 48. Eliot College looks bunker-like from its main approach, and the impression is emphasised by the brick out-crops on the roof. At the centre of the college there is a grassy open quadrangle, left, but this is one floor below the main level of circulation, and it is not heavily used.

49. *Darwin College has a Y-shaped plan, and the arms of the Y consist of two identical paved walkways at first floor level, with student rooms on both sides.*

simple functional plan, bi-symmetrical in the shape of a Y, with lecture rooms at the junction of the arms, and dining and social facilities in the stem. Although the physical form has changed markedly from the 1963 pattern, the concept remains the same: 'Our colleges have been created to grow into human-scale communities . . . they must be economically viable and socially possible,' wrote Dr Templeman to members of the university in 1970. Whilst Lord James chose the figure of 300 for his college size at York, Dr Templeman chose 600 from the beginning, and the real significance of this figure is to be found in some of the unitary universities, for when it is exceeded (in schools of studies, departments or whatever) the social structure begins to fall apart. Because of financial pressures, this decision, though made with great foresight, may now return to plague the inventor. The University Grants Committee norms, and their desire to see Kent reach a total population of 4,000 by 1976, may mean that with finance unavailable to build more colleges to the same standard of amenity, the existing colleges may have to be extended (a difficult assignment with a symmetrical plan) or worse still, re-arranged internally to cater for 1,000 students each. This result may appear to be efficient in economic terms but it may destroy a coherent society unit by transforming it into an unwieldy monster to which the individual finds it difficult to relate. In 1968, just before the opening of the third college, when part of the existing community was hived off, the first two coped with an undergraduate membership of 750 each. The UGC norms suggest that without alteration they could accommodate 850. With financial plans for the quinquennium beginning in 1972 still unclear, Kent—like York—must face the prospect of purely residential accommodation outside the college structure, built on the main site.

The registrar, Eric Fox, said in early 1971, '. . . the probability is that we are going to have to select parts of the site in which cheap building not more than two or three floors in height can be spread over a fairly wide area and still not look too bad'.[14] The financial stringency of the present day therefore has come to threaten the physical environment even of Kent, which rather goes to prove that refusing to have a master plan is not much of a consolation, when the squeeze comes.

The dozen or so major building groups on the site, dispersed by day under a wide sky and strangely united at night as campus lighting loops the buildings together, have every opportunity, as isolated units, to exhibit remarkable architectural invention. Without exception, however, they rely heavily on tradition in concept if not in structure, five of them being perfectly symmetrical: three of the colleges, the monumental library described in Chapter 5, and the Senate House.

This latter octagonal building, a mark of respectability like a seal on a charter, is sited so close to the massive library that it will always intrude into any view of the library's façade. It is one of the new small buildings by Farmer and Dark in the university's central area, together with the low quadrangular registry block and the Cornwallis building containing the computing laboratories and the language centre. These buildings depend for visual interest on the differing textures and shapes of cast concrete panels, but fail to rise above the utilitarian in appearance. At the west end of the Cornwallis building, however, are two halls, a large lecture room and a purpose-built theatre partly financed by a grant from the Gulbenkian foundation. Influenced by the economical Little Phoenix Theatre at Leicester, this attractive crystal-shaped auditorium (plate 50) was constructed for £70,000, and seats 342. With this potential, it strives to provide a link between the university and the city.

The science area begins to the west of the library with a low and well-appointed Physics building, the first to be built in 1964. The large Chemistry block is very close to the new Biology building and also nearby is the Sports Hall, designed by Faulkner Brown. This building, opened in 1966, accommodates two full-size tennis courts as well as the usual range of other indoor activities, and doubles as an examination hall. In the sports-centre stakes amongst the Seven, it must be the favourite, although it is rather awkwardly sited. One major building group lies farther to the west. It is Keynes, the third college, physically more separated from the rest of the university, and

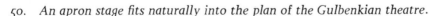

50. *An apron stage fits naturally into the plan of the Gulbenkian theatre.*

51, 52. Owl-like, the house of the master of Keynes College stands sentinel near the main entrance. The grey staircase towers, right, give the college a fortified appearance. Internally, much use is made of timber stained dark brown or bright red.

different in feeling. It draws on traditional academic architectural forms, and emphasises the staircase principle for its student residences. An original and arresting shape is used repeatedly for the staircase towers, providing a varied skyline (plate 52). Traditionalism in architecture is attractive to students, and this college, like County College at Lancaster, is the most popular.

The University of Kent was the last of the Seven to admit students, but when it did, in 1965, there were nearly 500 undergraduates in the first term, the largest initial intake of any university in Britain. They found on arrival a university-in-microcosm in a single new building with a way of life and an

academic structure, though broadly based, more traditional than elsewhere amongst the new universities.

In the first five years £7,500,000 was spent on buildings to extend the campus across its hilltop, and a viable community has emerged, numerically ahead of its original target. But aesthetically the campus has failed to achieve distinction in spite of some good buildings. And in spite of grassy terraces and criss-crossing concrete paths, it has not yet produced a coherent total environment, for it has no heart.

11 Essex

'The park is the most forward. The great difficulty has been to get so much in it as they wanted . . . My view comprehended too large a space. But today I have got over the difficulty and begin to like it myself.'[15] John Constable wrote this to his wife in 1816, while he was staying at Wivenhoe Park painting and to a certain extent *contriving* the landscape for his patron. It was this park which became, nearly 150 years later, the 204 acre site of Essex University. The landscape has been grasped, partially obliterated, and drawn into a deliberate counterpoint with man-made structures in the most uncompromising environment among the Seven. The seventeenth-century redbrick mansion of Constable's painting* still stands, surrounded by trees, though now modified and occupied by a limb of the university. The configuration of the artificial lakes is the same, but a third one has been created and across the dam shown in Constable's picture has been built the house of the Vice-Chancellor, Dr. Albert Sloman.

In 1963 Dr Sloman delivered the Reith Lectures, 'A University in the Making,' and in the minds of the general public he is more directly associated with the planning of a new university than other vice-chancellors. Both the structure and intent of Essex University are documented in some detail, thanks to these lectures, and the reality can be compared to the ideal. It was in response to Dr Sloman's concept of a university and the possibilities of the site that Kenneth Capon of the Architects' Co-Partnership produced a plan for Essex later in 1963. Like East Anglia and Lancaster, it is an urban concept striking in terms of originality and bravery, but by 1971, when a large chunk of the university had been built and used, it was beginning to emerge as an environment rather frigid in practice. The flexibility of the non-specialised buildings contrasts with the geometry of the purpose-built blocks, and in the continuous

* Wivenhoe Park, Essex, 1816. National Gallery of Washington.

◁ 53. *Not a range of buildings on a hillside, but the corner of a quadrangle, with rooms for teaching and research (physics) forming the sides.*

folded ribbon of buildings every unit, like cells in an animal or plant, seems to have a common set of master instructions, so that the university can only grow in accordance with its pre-determined genetic pattern.

Essex was revolutionary in making provision from the start for a very large university (up to 20,000) and the architect's first scheme was for 6,000, to be realised towards the end of the 1970s. The dense urban plan was intended to avoid a dispersed and straggling community (like that of Warwick) in the initial period, and pedestrian and wheeled traffic were to be separated on to two different levels. It was felt that in view of the nature of the courses at Essex University (each student starting with the study of several subjects from four overlapping schools) it would be inappropriate to build separate 'faculty' blocks, physically distinct. As a non-collegiate university, it was decided to integrate as much as possible the extra-curricular lives of the students with their working environment by making rooms for social purposes in the teaching buildings.

By concentrating the buildings together in one place, it was hoped to retain the park-like character of the Wivenhoe Estate. The university was therefore built in a small area in the valley below Wivenhoe House. The complex of buildings does not really lie *in* the valley; it obliterates it. A series of concrete piazzas is raised twenty-five feet above the valley on cylindrical concrete piles and around these are arranged teaching buildings, similarly supported, some of them extending sideways, at right angles to the 'spine', into the slopes of the valley sides. Farther away on each side, and farther up the slopes, are the residential tower blocks, the only major buildings which are separated one from the next, and which have the kind of physical integrity and relationship with their surroundings which one takes for granted with buildings in the country.

The little valley has become a white concrete town, inward-looking because of its piazzas, bunker-like when seen from the park because of its low position and the lack of height amongst its buildings. The body of the buildings inhales and exhales students and staff to the residential towers to left and right and ingests and discharges its physical needs through the service road built under the piazzas, where a little tributary of the River Colne used to run. Above the service road, the university buildings offer a total town environment in which the student can forget he is in the country.

Criticism of the environment is very widespread, and the totality of the planner's operations somewhere fails to connect on the human level. The same urban environment occurs at Lancaster, but there it has a less daunting scale and is more acceptable. At Essex there is something of the unreality of a row of shops on an ocean liner—a town in the middle of a park. The trees in Wivenhoe Park are carefully preserved, and tree-planting and lawn-making are going on in some areas, but the irony of this is that the trees are scarcely seen by the students, who complain of the bleakness of the concrete and glass which surrounds them in the squares. The commonest complaints about the architectural setting are not specific ones, such as the corridors being too narrow or the door knobs too high, but general ones, especially the lack of privacy. The inward-looking glazing faces the square courtyards in which there are no nooks and corners, and students have a sense of being under observation by their fellows whenever they are around the campus. Of course, there is a good deal of park to walk around in, but the forced contiguity within the

54. *The plain entrance to 'square 2', always busy with students during term time. At the centre of the square, right, four jets of water rising from a trough form the plainest fountain in English architecture. When the wind blows, the water does not land in the trough, and the jets are turned down.*

valley brings people into contact with each other regularly and often. The architect, Kenneth Capon, when confronted with criticism (usually that the environment is over-planned and not working) answers in effect, 'wait until it is finished and you will see it all fall into place'. It is therefore sad that his grand plan, like Lasdun's at Norwich, will probably never be completed. His mandate continues until 1972, but thereafter depends upon a continuing flow of capital which is unlikely to materialise, and the expensive high-rise accommodation, so important a feature of his plan, will be the first casualty.

Right at the beginning, the concrete squares above the valley spine were erected, and looked like concrete tables on dowel legs, which may account for their official name of podia or 'raised platforms'—rather misleading as when they are finished and have buildings around the edges, they become enclosed piazzas known in the university as Square 3, Square 4, etc. They have effectively created a new ground level, or at least a waterline. Down below, in the cavernous service area, the burly windowless concrete shapes of departmental blocks are identified in stencilled lettering as 'Chemistry Department', etc., like names painted low on the hulls of ships to help the diver about his business in an otherwise undifferentiated gloom. The five squares are staggered in a mild zigzag, following the line of the old river and following its downward progress too, for there are two changes of level, each of about 12 feet, between Square 2 and Square 3, and Square 3 and Square 4. Through the rectangular and undecorated opening made by the interconnections there is, looking up the valley, a persistent view of Wivenhoe House. When the series of five piazzas is complete in 1972, the main entrance will be by the

55. From his room overlooking a quadrangle, a lecturer at Essex can see nothing of Wivenhoe Park, only the concrete mullions of the windows opposite, arranged in permutations which conceal the regular grid of the structure.

lower road and the visitor will pop up, rubbing his eyes, in the heart of the complex in Square 3.

Each square is slightly dished, with a rectangular feature in its centre—a fountain or a compass rose in mosaic—and to stand in one of them on a sunny day is painful to the eyes, for both pavement and walls are white. Few enclosed spaces in towns are so completely empty of something-that-grows, but trees cannot be planted here for the squares are only platforms like biscuit-tin lids and the roots would dangle in space above the service road below. Shallow flower beds have not been attempted, and the harshness of the squares is abrasive. A university society called The Concrete Tree was formed in 1969, dedicated to the softening of the buildings with living plants, but so far the only concession has been a gift of flower pots from the architect himself. Inside the research and teaching rooms philodendrons and Tradescantia thrive, brought in by teachers and technicians who wanted to soften their immediate surroundings.

To the south of Square 2 and the north of Square 3 are open-terraced amphitheatres which follow the line of the valley sides and are enclosed by the Physics and Social Studies buildings respectively. The terraces have been used for teaching and open-air entertainment and are shown in plate 53. In keeping with the designer's intention, the buildings which surround these amphitheatres and the squares are similar in appearance and interchangeable in function. They are general teaching buildings designed to a module, but with pre-cast panels on the exterior so full of variables that a vertical mood is obtained in the façades without an impression of repetition. The exposed ends of the concrete transverse beams project like corbels (plate 55). The same size of building houses Chemistry, Physics, the Language Centre, Economics, etc., and Essex, like East Anglia, attempts to accommodate these different disciplines in complete architectural uniformity.

The purpose-built units lie on either side of the central spine and consist of the library, restaurant, lecture blocks and residential towers. The library is at the extremity of the central university site and in its present form has

56. *The library. Four reading floors overhang the administrative floor and bookshop.*

◁ *57, 58. The hallway of the lecture block, left, is a popular congregating area. The creosoted timber roof is supported by concrete corbels, leaving a 'pathway' of glazing round the edge. The large lecture room, above, includes a translators' gallery.*

four floors of book stacks and reading places for 700. As the university population approaches 3,000 the library's capacity will be reached, and a doubling
of its size by a northwards extension is planned, but this will not help to make
it any more central. Around the foot of the library on the south-east side, and
below piazza level, is the Auditorium, an experimental area with a large re-
arrangeable stage for dramatic and musical activities—a clear indication of
Essex University's intention to provide student facilities for creative work as
well as research.

While the library windows stare wide-eyed over the campus, the hexagonal
restaurant, or 'Hex', is inward-looking and almost totally windowless. Day-
light comes from a hexagonal glass structure in the roof, and the symmetry
of the building is as pure as a carbon ring. Standing in the current of student
movement from residential to working areas, and amidst buildings which are
brilliant white when the sun shines, it is gloomy and dull, a chunk of basalt.
Each face has two symmetrical glass slits amidst vertical panes of pre-cast dark
grey concrete. It can thus claim to be a 'sanctuary' area in a campus rather
preoccupied with over-exposure. Inside there is something of the air of a big
top, a feeling of warmth common in circular buildings with few windows, like
the Round House in London. It is often surprising how many people non-
rectangular buildings will hold; here 500 diners or 1,500 lunches in a two-hour
spell. The hexagonal principle is extended to the shape of the tables, which
is practical and good for social reasons; only the access to the servery is dis-
appointing, together with the quality of the food. There is a more luxurious
restaurant in Square 3, and another in Wivenhoe House.

Like the Hexagon restaurant, the main lecture block lies outside the spine
of the university, and again like the Hexagon it has obtuse angles in abundance. But this time it is far from regular. Designed by Cadbury-Brown and
Partners, it is widely liked by students and staff and consists of interlocking
faceted cells, with a large assembly area the full height of the building. This
fine space is shown in plate 57 and a lecture hall in plate 58. In the two
larger lecture rooms a common wall can be moved aside to provide a single

59. *If you press the button on the fifteenth floor, and the lift has just gone, it can be quite a long wait. The two lifts in each residential block share a common 'memory' and take calls in downward sequence to aid the evacuation of the building at rush hours. Students nervous of heights are found rooms on the lower floors.*

hall accommodating a thousand people, for degree days and other ceremonies. Unfortunately, background noise in the lecture block is high because of generators sited nearby, and there are other distractions, as the most popular entrance to the university passes the side of the lecture block, and students walking to and from the new residential towers have taken the place of builders' wheelbarrows as objects of interest seen through the windows.

The residential towers, housing in 1970 over 1,000 students within two hundred yards of the university's heart, are the most obvious example of commitment to concentration at Essex. No alternative is provided for the living-in student. Dr Sloman devoted one of his Reith Lectures to the problems of student residences, and the towers of Essex have been a focusing point for criticism and research. It *is* revolutionary to build high brick towers where there is space to house students in lower buildings, without the need for lifts and special plumbing. It was, in 1963, running contrary to established opinion to build blocks of flats for students of both sexes with no supervision and no common rooms, when halls of residence were regarded as the only satisfactory solution. A major innovation was the degree of independence and autonomy amongst students. 'The best way to make them responsible,' said Dr Sloman, '. . . is to give them responsibility.'[16] The interlayering of male and female floors, rather than the sexual segregation of the towers, has been a success, but the provision of working space for non-resident 'members' of a flat has not, and the vice-chancellor amongst others regrets that this experiment will not be continued in new residential schemes for the university.

In spite of its plans for great growth, Essex University has stuck closer than the rest of the Seven to its projected targets, and in its first seven years has grown to a strength of nearly 2,000 students—and has gained something of a reputation for outspoken behaviour and self-criticism. The tight, urban, concentrated appearance is tied in with the academic approach. Though the valley site allows the university to orientate itself towards Colchester, links between the town and the university could grow a great deal closer. The grey residential towers are gloomy and menacing from a distance, and are, unfortunately, all the average townsman sees of the university.

The familiar irregular vertical ribbing of the pre-cast window panels in the teaching blocks (plate 53) and the post-and-lintel arcades around the squares make Essex at close quarters seem to be one of the most modern of the Seven, but it is harsh and stark, and many of the members of the university react against it, as well as being conditioned by it. Essex University is proud of its Wivenhoe site, and yet in creating an inward-looking town it appears to reject its landscape advantages.

60. *This is the view many students at Essex have of their university—from high up a residential tower. And the urban campus in Wivenhoe Park does not look its best from above. In the picture can be seen the hexagonal restaurant, centre right, with four tower blocks beyond. The lecture block complex is in the foreground.*

61. *Flat-topped and slab-sided, the library with the science block behind shows the characteristic image of Warwick University.*

104

12 Warwick

Warwick University, three miles from Coventry and twelve miles from Warwick, is hidden in 400 acres of parkland, fringed with trees. The story of the
development of this campus in its beautiful setting is one of false starts and
broken tiles, of a physical environment far from satisfactory in spite of much-
praised buildings by its several architects, and a lack of co-ordination and
completeness which is bound to stay with it for some time to come.

When the foundation was approved by the UGC, Arthur Ling (Chief Architect to the city of Coventry) prepared a master plan in association with Alan
Goodman. Like the Essex and East Anglia plans, the scale of their university
was much greater than the UGC recommendation of 3,000 in ten years, and it
was conceived as a university town with 20,000 students, reaching out towards
Coventry and finally linking with it. The Ling and Goodman plan was far-
sighted in organising the vehicle highways in line with projected future needs
and, like several of its fellows, it depended upon a pedestrian spine in the
form of glazed arcades. In developing the theme of linear planning, this
vertebrate scheme was the still-born brother of the successful plan at Lancaster. Each of the over-ambitious schemes has fallen short of its hopes, and
Warwick most of all—for the great scheme was abandoned as demanding too
large a share of available government money when Arthur Ling left Coventry
for Nottingham.

It is tempting to regret what was forestalled, and to extol the virtues of a
plan which never had to stand the crucial test of experience, but if, as suggested in Chapter 2, just one of the Seven had been intended from the start to
be a giant university, it might most naturally have been Warwick, at the
heart of Britain. If so, the original plan might have suited very well, for
although the scheme was ambitious it was not wasteful, and the emphasis in
the present decade on the intensive use of facilities suggests that a university
town on the scale planned by Ling and Goodman would have been good value
today, had it been built in the 1960s.

A neat and small-scale instalment of the first development plan had been

62, 63. *A lecture theatre is an inclined slab on one side of a quadrangle at the East site. The sensitive arrangement of forms and the small scale of these buildings designed by Grey, Goodman and Partners makes them popular. A staircase block is shown right.*

built on a part of the original site by Grey, Goodman and Partners while the main scheme was under discussion, and it became the centre for the university when it opened in 1965 (plates 62 and 63). Consisting of lecture halls, teaching rooms, social areas, refectory and administration block, it was a good environment for the first 425 students. Apart from a cluster of staff residences, it has not been extended since, although several of the buildings have been rearranged internally to provide a flexible 'nursery' for new departments before they move to the main site. Its main function today is as an administrative outlier on its island site, half a mile away from the main acreage.

The second plan for the main campus was prepared by Yorke Rosenberg and Mardall, who were appointed consultant architects in 1963. This firm produced a less inventive scheme although, significantly, the ultimate size of the university was still to be large—20,000. An essentially rectilinear grid was proposed to cover the gently sloping farmland, dividing the site up into blocks like the plan of an American town. The model prepared by the consultant architects must have shocked many, with its vistas of wide parallel roads flanked by low rectangular slab-sided buildings, and its vast impersonal scale. Kafkaesque students could be imagined, bewildered amongst the blind façades and endless avenues. Two roads, each 1,000 yards long, were to cross the site by the time the population had reached 10,000, and the model showed no sign that these impersonal routeways would be broken up to reassure the viewer or dissuade the prevailing wind.

It is hard to see the need for so regular a grid, ignoring the natural undulations of the land. In fact, however, the site-works necessary to make the roads forming this framework were phased, and all but the very first one have been postponed so that, unlike Lancaster and York, the university has to rely for access on a narrow country lane, Gibbet Hill Road, which has always wandered across the site. Thus in the absence of major roads, it is the buildings themselves, begun on the main site in 1964, which uphold the rectilinear scheme, lining up to toe an invisible line.

A major decision affecting the environment of the campus was the zoning of areas for certain functions, with residence kept firmly at a distance from teaching areas and administration. It was therefore the antithesis of the collegiate concept such as exists at York. The separation of teaching, living, service and recreation areas by wide tracts of open land which would only gradually be built over seems defiantly designed to encourage entrenched positions between establishment and student body instead of promoting harmony and integration. 'The first generations of students were to be cheerfully sacrificed in the name of the plan and the cause of expansion,' wrote Edward Thompson in 1970,[17] and indeed the spaces and the dispersal of the units give the very sense of incompleteness to the environment which the other universities tried hard to avoid. In addition, the campus was made especially vulnerable to financial cutbacks of the kind that have occurred since 1965.

The architecture of the university is so big that it is de-humanised. The colleges at York, designed for units of 300 people, wiggle about in plan and gradually unfold, concealing their scale from the visitor. At Warwick, the buildings emphasise their great bulk with smooth façades which do little to make the student warm to his environment, and the only noticeable policy relating numbers of users to buildings seems to be 'make it bigger'.

When the student first comes to Warwick he sees a low range of cold grey

64. *Windows and glazed white tiles on the walls of the library. At close quarters the discolouration of the tiles can be seen.*

buildings with a perfectly horizontal skyline, reminiscent of an industrial estate. His first impression of the university is bound to be affected by the architects' choice of white glazed tiles for cladding. These tiles, beautiful at close range, and grouted like graph paper with black cement, are cold and impersonal when seen from a distance, and the tile unit is too small to make an effective surface pattern on tall buildings. As all the early buildings on the main site used this cladding, however, the impact on the campus as a whole is considerable, as can be seen in the accompanying plates.

With the Midlands' tradition for brick, and the abundance of iron-rich limestone, the university site might have responded more enthusiastically to a warmer surface material, but it is for technical reasons that the tile cladding has proved most unsatisfactory. Square yards at a time have come clattering down to break on the concrete paths beneath, because of a mysterious fault in the bonding. The precise cause is still unknown, but in view of the danger to life and limb, the immediate surroundings of the buildings have had to be cordoned off with picket fences to deter sunbathers or mere walkers from approaching too close to the walls. This practical fault in the cladding means that the tiles have been abandoned, and as more buildings in the campus rise up in the spaces, the chilling effect on the appearance of the university will become progressively less. In 1972 they still dominate the two main areas: the teaching block and the residential halls.

Two broad Boards of Studies, one for arts and one for sciences, govern the academic structure at Warwick, and their respective schools or departments are housed in massive buildings with a new main road separating them, underlining the old division of the 'two cultures'. A continuous tile-clad complex to the north contains Physics, Engineering Science and Molecular Sciences, and nearby is the Computer Centre. Six storeys high, the sciences block is linked at first floor level by a pedestrian bridge (plate 65) to the large library block.

65. *Entrance to the library across the pedestrian bridge or from the road is by way of the two-storey gatehouse block, which contains rooms for private study.*

66, 67, 68. The social building, above, containing the Airport Lounge, right. The heaters in metal sleeves which run around the edge of this building are exactly at eye level for anyone sitting down, and they effectively cut out the most interesting part of the view. Below right is the staircase hall.

This bridge is the only part of the proposed pedestrian routeway to have been built.

A formidable block from the outside, built from the start to cater for 5,000 students, the library is well-appointed and efficient within, and includes amongst its varied seating options waist-high carrels which are popular and unique within the Seven. The library won an RIBA award in 1967.

Close to the eastern end of the library is the enormous Arts building which, though tile clad, differs from its neighbours by the lack of major vertical divisions in the fenestration. It has a series of horizontal stripes, black and white like a liquorice allsort, and there is no significant entrance to break the purity of its north-eastern façade. To the east of this block is the newly-completed sports hall.

A broad dome of open land separates these buildings from the residential area, five minutes' walk away. The original intention was to build ranks of study-bedrooms and separate 'social buildings' for each of several student halls. With planned communities of 1,000 students, the Warwick halls hold the record for mere size amongst the Seven, although they were never intended as colleges.

In fact, the social building for the first hall, Rootes Hall, built in 1966, has had to act much as a students' union for the whole university, for similar facilities have not yet been provided for the second hall built alongside in 1968. The social building is the nerve centre for student activity at Warwick, and contains refectory, shops, bars and offices as well as a big open room on the first floor nicknamed 'the Airport Lounge' (plate 67). Students complaining of waste space in the planning of this building often quote the broad staircase hall (plate 68) as an example, but in practice it is effective and popular as a place for meeting and mixing, eating and posting notices.

69. *Benefactor's Hall provides accommodation on a generous scale for one in twenty of the residents on the campus. The four façades of the building are identical, and at the top of the building are two-person two-level 'studios'.*

A well-appointed small residential block (plate 69) was built as a result of an American benefaction, but most of the 550 residential students of Rootes Hall are accommodated in the two terraces which face each other across a concrete path (plate 8). The Second Hall is rather more popular as a place to live, with better room planning and more grass and trees in the immediate surroundings, but it has the same depressing appearance of uniformity. Half the population of over 2,000 students is accommodated in these two halls and in the absence of anything else, they are the focus of the fragmented campus.

The expectations of students and staff who hope to find at Warwick a stimulating environment are dampened by the architecture. It was a demand by students for action on the part of the buildings committee which led in the spring of 1970 to a band of students marching from the social building up Gibbet Hill Road to East Site. Here, in the registry, took place the first of a series of sit-ins which led to the 'incident of the files', and dissatisfaction was very widespread.

In autumn 1970, Yorke Rosenberg and Mardall resigned as consultant architects and Warwick University was once more in search of a plan. Three groups of buildings—the East Site, a living area and a teaching area—were the inheritance, together with a vestigial road system. In 1971 a single building, the Arts Centre, designed by Renton, Howard, Wood Associates, was being built as a link between the living and teaching areas, and sited *at an angle* in an attempt to break the deadlock of the rectilinear plan.

In February 1971 a new step was taken in the development of this least happy of campuses when the architectural consultancy was taken over by Shepheard and Epstein, designers of the successful University of Lancaster.

70, 71. *Most of the rooms in Rootes Hall, above, are identical, and are comfortably furnished though not spacious. A contrast in housing is shown below, computer-age housing for visiting members of the staff at the Mathematics Research Centre. This cluster of houses is an appendage to the East site.*

72.   On its plateau site at Bailrigg, Lancashire, the campus of Lancaster University looks uncannily like a Mediterranean hilltop town. Prominent is the bulging shape of the Chaplaincy Centre with its trefoil of chapels, and to the right is the fourteen-storey residence block, Bowland Tower. Cars from the A6 must follow a winding road, but pedestrians can walk straight up the hill.

13 Lancaster

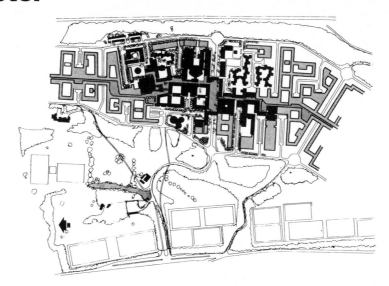

'Lancaster is not set in a remote fastness of difficult access,' says the introduction to the university prospectus, and indeed it would seem that excellence of communication in all its forms has been one of the top priorities in the development of this glistening Lancastrian campus on its hillside site. From the orderly and detailed prospectus itself, running to 232 pages, to its internal telephone network; from the university bus service to the encouragement it gives outsiders to enquire and be answered, the university seems to be a well-oiled piece of machinery.

Michael Beloff, in searching for one word to sum up the spirit of Lancaster, chose 'efficiency',[18] but this implies inhumanity, and a major asset of Lancaster is its environmental success in human terms.

The last of the Seven to be approved, moving to its main site in 1966 and admitting its first residential students only in 1968, Lancaster is growing quickly and is now second only to Sussex in size among the new universities. Anxious for self-enlargement, its territorial claims will make it vaster even than Warwick when it straddles the M6 motorway to Hazelrigg. Nevertheless, Lancaster has achieved a degree of contentment within its environment, a lack of growing pains which other universities should envy. Some of the credit for this lies in the adherence to a combination of traditional and radical principles—it shares its collegiate traditionalism with Kent and York, whereas much of its radicalism lies in the master plan for a university town, inviting comparison with East Anglia and Essex. But the innovations are unobtrusive, and the atmosphere is one of calm.

The new foundation of Lancaster—provided with a 200 acre site three miles from Lancaster by the Lancaster City Council in 1963—asked Gabriel Epstein of Shepheard and Epstein to produce such a plan, and his proposal was stylishly simple. Assuming the need to integrate buildings closely, to mix social, residential and teaching areas intimately, to encourage extra-curricular activity and evening participation, and to separate vehicular and pedestrian traffic, Epstein proposed a 'vertebrate' plan, with a pedestrian spine. Like Essex and

73. *There is always someone crossing Alexandra Square, which is central and the largest open space inside the campus. A long rectangle fringed with shops, the paving of this square forms the roof of the underpass below. On the right is the library; in the centre, Bowland Tower, cloaking the boiler house chimney, and on the left, Bowland College. The steps face south, and are crowded on sunny days.*

East Anglia, and the early plan for Warwick, it was to be an 'urban' community. The pedestrian spine was deliberately narrow, reducing to 18 feet in places, encouraging if not congestion at least concentration. As at Essex, vehicular access to the university's centre is by a subterranean tunnel, but a key difference is that while at Essex the road runs along below the pedestrian way and parallel to it, at Lancaster it is at right angles. The pedestrian spine runs north-south, the underpass east-west. The significance of this lies in the fact that the ancillary feeder roads also run east-west, in a series of cul-de-sacs or tongues running at ground level up to the spine, penetrating deep into the university and allowing the campus to 'breathe'.

By making the pedestrian spine the centre of gravity of the university, and building progressively away from it in ribs, activities near the centre can be carried on without the disconcerting awareness of building operations and noise. There is a perimeter road to the site sufficiently far away from the spine to allow all buildings to grow like branches of a tree, while at regular intervals the cul-de-sacs come as close as 50 feet to the spine itself.

The module of 35 foot wide buildings, 100 foot wide college 'quads', and 100 foot wide interstitial spaces for the access roads and parking is carefully maintained. Gabriel Epstein has said, 'If we don't maintain the grid we will lose control of the total development and will not be able to maximise the use of the site'. Density is at stake, of course, but so are the university's aesthetics. An aesthetic guide line has been the horizontal feeling of the university, given expression without any difficulty by the recurrent horizontality of the covered ways. This horizontality recurs in the first and second storeys of the surrounding buildings and in particular in the accented line of the top of the second storey. Above this, the architects Shepheard and Epstein urge 'unusual shapes' at rooftop level to counteract the depression of horizontals and to ensure a lively skyline. The monoclinal roof motif invented by Gabriel Epstein (plate 76), using lift towers, water storage tanks and any appropriate excrescences as subjects, is an effective foil to the lower storey lines. Painted white, it contrasts with the golden brick of the rest of the buildings. The other five architects involved in the campus have respected Epstein's requests with regard to either colour or roof motifs, but without studiously copying them.

Lancaster University does not look impressive from the road. Its setting is a magnificent green and grey landscape, stretching as far as the eye can see, and on a clear winter's day including the snow-topped hills to the east. From the approach road, the low buildings on their hill are dominated by the bulging curve of the Chaplaincy Centre, with its trefoil of circular chapels (plate 72). Its forward position gives it great prominence and conveys an impression of unusual emphasis on religion, although the building of this Chaplaincy Centre is the result of enthusiasm from the churches, not pressure from the university. Perhaps the combination of chapel and playing fields encountered on approach give the campus a boarding-school ethos, which I must confess I find strengthened rather than otherwise by the smooth-running organisation of the campus as a whole.

The perimeter road—kidney-shaped, with the underpass as its waist—encompasses a tight mass of sturdy buildings and an abundance of car parking places. There are no vast hillside car parks as at Essex and Sussex, and 1,250 cars can be accommodated in small groups with ease. Once inside the university, small trees, small shops and low covered walkways remove any sense of awe from the architecture, even in Alexandra Square under the eye of the fourteen-storey Bowland Tower.

In the main the standards of finish at Lancaster are good. The impression that the bread-and-butter buildings are mainly bread with the butter thinly spread is perhaps something to do with the construction of the covered walkways. Unlike the repeating units at Sussex University—massive cast concrete segmental arches—the spindly wooden supports of the walkways at Lancaster give an impression of flimsiness, and the varnished softwood ceiling finish one of sparse means. Plate 74 shows clearly how the 'covered' ways have been left carefully *uncovered* for half of their width, providing a sunny side to walk along when the weather is good. Just as the covered area switches sides to provide variety, so the buildings flanking the pedestrian way have been carefully alternated so that no two high buildings come close together and walkway never turns into gloomy defile. Indeed, although the pathway narrows in places, it also widens into open areas of concrete or grass. To either side lie the colleges and teaching buildings in close sequence.

74. *Overleaf: Patches of sunlight and shadow change sides in the partially covered* ▷ *pedestrian spine which runs the length of the campus from north to south, but is carefully varied in width. Opposite the chemistry department is the refectory of Lonsdale College, and, farther along, the entrance to the Faraday lecture halls.*

As at York and Kent the colleges are intended to give the student a sense of belonging to a comprehensible unit, even when the university has grown large. It is the intention that they should not exceed a total of more than 600 students each and new colleges have been founded and added as the numbers have grown, so that by 1972 there are seven. There will never be a large central students' union building, as social and recreational facilities are provided in each college. Because the colleges merge physically one into the next the isolation so strongly felt at Kent is not apparent here, and as all college facilities such as refectories and bars are open to everyone, a supply-and-demand law governs the services provided. An over-lavish provision of catering facilities results in some college kitchens lying unused while students go to eat in neighbouring college canteens and yet a tidal wave of students all demanding lunch in one place is avoided. The policy of college rather than centralised catering keeps refectories small and intimate, and dog-leg planning as in the bars makes them seem even smaller and more friendly.

The first two colleges to be built, Bowland and Lonsdale, are twins, each consisting of an elongated quadrangle divided by a long low lecture block in the centre, creating two squares of modest size. The three-storey blocks forming the walls of the quadrangle are a mixture of teaching, social and private rooms. On the top floor are flats for academic staff, set back from the façade on both sides like the top (servants') storey of eighteenth-century houses in London, but rather more comfortably arranged. Almost everyone is delighted on arriving at roof level to find himself in a new and unexpected world with a very intimate appeal (plate 75). Whilst Lonsdale College takes under its skirts a small grassy quadrangle to the north, Bowland College extends across the top of Alexandra Square and includes the fourteen-storey tower, which cloaks a 100 foot high chimney from the university's boilerhouse. High-rise living is not a matter of principle at Lancaster, but some 100 students live in the tower and look down on the university from its geographical centre. Built in warm yellow brick, with balcony, window surroundings and superstructure in white, the unassuming tower has a nautical air, like the funnel of a newly painted ship. From the top of this residential tower the plan of the university can clearly be seen.

Attached to the Physics and Chemistry buildings to the east of the pedestrian spine is the Faraday lecture block. Its three lecture halls, one large, two smaller, serve all departments of the university. The cluster of apse-like bays which face outwards towards the pedestrian way are merely for standing about in before and after lectures, and the whole helps to soften the approach to the inevitable bulk of the science building behind.

Continuing along the spine on the north side is Cartmel College, assigned to architects Taylor, Young and Partners and designed by Haydn Smith. Intended in the first place to maintain the spirit of the first two colleges, it was as a result of a financial accident that Haydn Smith's design caused a revolution

75, 76. A simple monoclinal roof motif is used in many variations throughout the ▷ *Lancaster campus to create a lively skyline. In the lower picture it is seen from footpath level in one of the quadrangles of Bowland College. One emerges at roof-top level into a surprising new world. The white painted cement faces of the recessed top floor create an attractive environment for academic staff flats. Above, Furness College, looking north.*

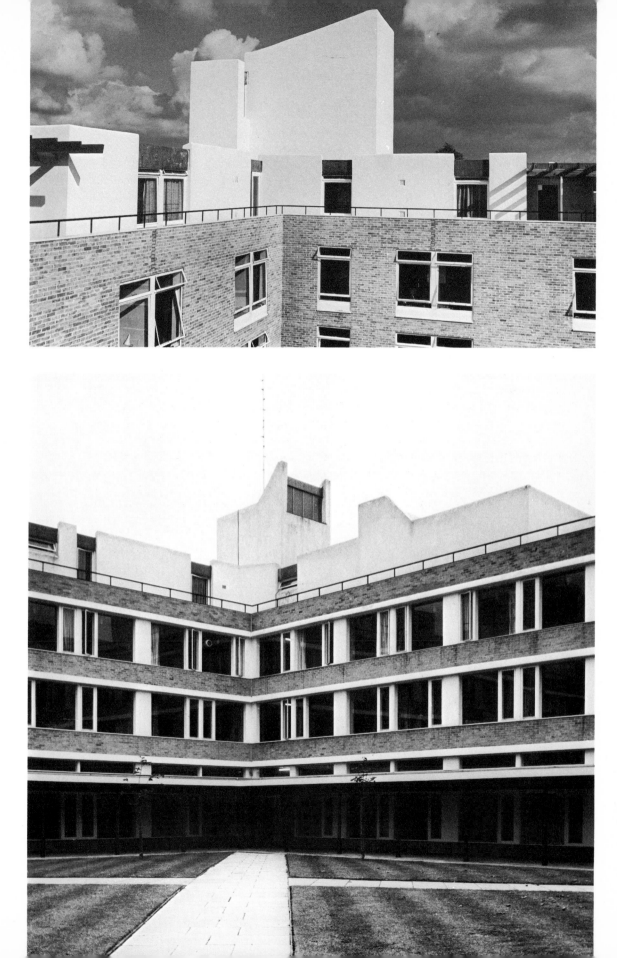

at Lancaster which has echoed across the campuses of all expanding universities. Financial support ran out as the original quadrangle plan was nearing completion, and the college was left with inadequate accommodation and no residential space. Using a building society loan, the architect plugged the open end of the U-shaped college with the now famous low-cost housing units described in Chapter 4 (plate 9).

Each block is approached by a separate footpath and though sharing a common wall, the blocks are not intercommunicating. The success of these extremely popular living quarters lies in a numerical relationship which builds up a sound social structure—the block unit of thirty-two is a useful intermediate stage between the floor unit of ten or eleven and the college residential total of around three hundred.

Variety of accommodation at Lancaster is very apparent and if the low-unit-cost housing is now triumphantly extended to Furness and Fylde Colleges at the south-eastern end of the spine, then a formidable rival for favour lies at the extreme northern end of the site: County College. A benefaction of £500,000 from the County of Lancashire was made for the foundation of a residential college. The university entrusted its design to the Lancashire county architects' office, and from the hands of Roger Booth came a design differing both aesthetically and technically from the rest of the campus. Notwithstanding the Bowland Tower and the Chaplaincy Centre, it is by far the most 'monumental' of the Lancaster buildings. Although it uses a pre-cast building technique, it is also by far the most traditional university building in concept. Arranged around an old oak tree, its structural antecedents lie in New College Oxford and in St John's College Cambridge. It is a honeycomb of student 'cells'; it is paved with magnificent textured slate, giving instant age; it has an entrance 'arch' with heavy iron gates and a porter's lodge with slit-window, functioning like a relic 'gatehouse' on a fifteenth-century castle. It even has a couple of postern gateways, emblazoned with the college arms. The interior is pseudo-cloister, glazed, and repeating cast units not unlike a Tudor arch transport the intruder far away from the Lancashire hillside into an academic enclave, persuading new materials (concrete) and modern techniques (casting) to counterfeit the ancient handwriting of academic architecture. No committed architectural radical could tolerate this building, but its prima donna quality makes it irresistible to almost everyone else.

Immediately it came into occupation in 1969 it ousted Bowland College as the most popular choice amongst applicants for a place at Lancaster University. Undoubtedly the physical appeal of the buildings (plates 78 to 80) has much to do with this choice, and several students I spoke to had come to Lancaster, seen County College, and put their name down for it without further search. The college respects the 'building thickness' module of 35 feet, and a simple continuous plan on second, third and fourth floor level consists of a central corridor, rather monastic with heavy doors, off which lead identical students' rooms, with services, access and a communal living space called a 'mixing-bay' at each corner of the building. The deep-relief cast units, clearly seen on page 124, which form the glazed 'end' to each student's room are attractive from inside, and add about a foot to the room's depth. The glazing to the corner mixing-bay is on the outside of the college only and the large sheets of plate glass which form a prominent stripe down the building at each corner always look streaked and unclean as well as revealing disorder inside—the

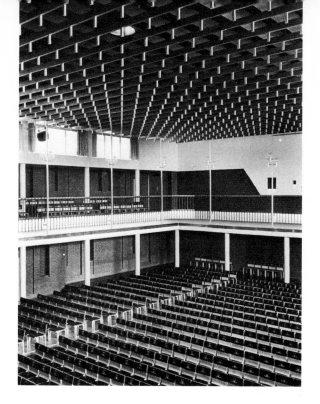

77. *The Great Hall has a balcony on three sides, and its rear wall is lined with acoustic brick. It was intended that the design of the ceiling should make the attachment of temporary decorations an easy matter.*

squalor of the mixing-bays seems particularly exposed to the world by the plate-glass windows. Thick black rubber coverings on stairways, and mahogany panelling where internal pre-cast units are infilled to make walls (plate 80) give a feeling of luxury not common at the new universities.

Near the large grey mass of County College is the circular Visual Aids Department, an island building contrasting in its roundness with the heavy masses of a cluster of halls to the west. Using clerestory or other forms of over-head lighting, these buildings are stark from the exterior with many plain wall surfaces. Internally, the Great Hall—for concerts and examinations—has a permanently festive appearance, with its many-celled wooden ceiling and balcony reminding one of an old fashioned music-hall. The smaller Jack Hylton memorial music rooms evoke even more the auditoria of another age. These buildings are clearly modern and new, but they maintain a happy link with the tradition of theatrical architecture. A large Barbara Hepworth sculpture stands to one side of the entrance way which these two halls share from the peripheral road.

On the other side of the same complex of buildings are the fine-arts studios and the large Nuffield Theatre Workshop. The latter gives infinite variety in methods of staging and has massive lighting installations to cope with the permutations of rostra and audience. These creative departments may come to have a more germinal function in the university as projects such as Drama and Ceramics are drawn into the academic options open to the students.

No building in a university can be more germinal than the library. Lancaster University library, designed by Tom Mellor & Partners, is described in Chapter 5. Its central siting and inconspicuous entrance are much to be praised. The success of this building is in the functional efficiency of its interior. As it is lit by a central well, some external walls are featureless, like the blind wall which backs on to the pedestrian spine. This broad and dreary part of the spine

78, 79, 80.   *The hundred year old oak tree above is carefully preserved in the centre of County College. This mainly residential college, designed by Roger Booth, houses 312 students in individual 'cells', each with a pre-cast projecting window. Though glazed throughout, the visual pattern of the ground floor recalls the traditional cloister, and here the structural units are faced with Westmorland limestone. The magnificent dark textured paving stones, however, come all the way from Co Clare, Ireland. A slightly monastic air is carried through the interior by the pre-cast structural units seen in the junior common room, right, and in a typical corridor, above right. Internal walls are made of grey brick in the corridors and mahogany panelling elsewhere. But despite the high quality carpeting and fittings, sound insulation is poor. County College is equipped with a refectory which is not at present used, as catering patterns have moved towards self catering by students. It will, however, eventually be shared by other colleges when they are built, nearby.*

81. *Water falls musically into the copper trays of the fountain in the square quadrangle of Furness College. As in most of the courtyards at Lancaster, there is a covered way here, lined with varnished wood and detached from the main structure.*

between the library and the supermarket opposite is now roofed with translucent polyester, concave in shape, its framework held in place with pendant weights rather than trusses. It has become an ideal Speakers' Corner for meetings, protected from the Lancashire rain. Further south along the spine is the Environmental Studies building, also by Tom Mellor & Partners. And at the southern end of the spine is the same architects' sports centre.

Lancaster is more enthusiastic about sport than most of the Seven, and in the early non-residential days great efforts were made to promote on-campus activities by making facilities available. The sports centre, true to the New University archetype, provides for most sports in a multi-purpose court, and in addition there is table-tennis and squash, a mountaineering wall and even a sauna bath.

The sports centre is the extremity of the university campus at present. It hunches its shoulders against the cold winds from the sea, and the landscaping of the site (also by Shepheard and Epstein) includes much tree planting. The trees are not only in and among the campus buildings, but also act as a wind shield and protection around the southern end of the site. Over 20,000 trees have already been planted, and at the south-east end the artificial mound which is a motorway embankment on one side will become a woodland slope as fast as the trees can be made to grow on it.

In 1972 the first university building programme will be completed with the Engineering block alongside the sports centre. By 1976, both the UGC and the Vice-Chancellor, Charles Carter, anticipate total numbers approaching 5,000, and provision is being made for a further stage of expansion. Lancaster has been able to spend more than £2,000,000 from its successful appeals fund, but the university is dependent on the continuing flow of finance. It has made provision for its own future needs by buying a 150 acre farm—the Hazelrigg site on the far side of the M6 motorway—and the Barker House site adjacent to its Bailrigg campus, to add a further 90 acres to the west. These safety-valve areas for expansion are on the east and west, but perhaps expansion should be northwards instead, to approach the southward expansion of the city of Lancaster.

The roundabout at the eastern limit of the underpass is virtually on the embankment of the M6, making a bridge link with the Hazelrigg site a possibility. An extension in this direction would easily allow for a university of 20,000, as planned at Warwick, but it is hard to imagine how the two sides could ever overcome the schism of the motorway and form a single social unit. Meanwhile a university of 7,000 or 8,000, appoaching the size of Oxford or Cambridge, will fit comfortably within the existing peripheral road, as the plan on page 115 shows. To call it a snug fit is to imply that there is an air of complacency over Bailrigg which, I think, would be wrong. Continuous self-examination and good communications on all levels ensure growth under strict observation for the corporate body, but for the individual the environment allows liberty, and makes Lancaster University a good place to live and work. The urban concept based on a linear structure is much praised, and makes Lancaster a model for university plans in the future. But it is not the plan alone which brings success to this campus. The design of the buildings themselves, unpretentious yet striking, helps to make this campus a most remarkable one.

Acknowledgements

Essential in the preparation of this book was the information and comment so readily offered and given by students and members of staff at all the universities. To these many unnamed helpers I express my gratitude.

The book could not have been undertaken without the specialist help of architects, Building Officers, Surveyors and Estate Officers, and in particular I would like to thank Jim Thomas at Sussex, George Whipp at York, Gordon Marshall at East Anglia, David Edwards at Kent, Tony Linscott at Essex, Philip Wood at Warwick and Donald Smith at Lancaster. I should also like to thank The Architectural Press for permission to reproduce the university plans.

The many aspects of university planning are illuminated by those people whose function or whose responsibility helps to form the structure of the university, and I received much help from Dr Volker Berghahn, Mr Neil Chatfield, Professor Keith Clayton, Mr G. S. Darlow, Mr Harry Fairhurst, Mrs June Farrington, Miss Jean Felton, Miss Elizabeth Fudakowska, Mr Willi Guttsmann, Miss Joanna Hall, Dr David Harkness, Lord James, Dr Richard Keesing, Dr Dave King, Mr J. Mangold, Dr Paddy O'Toole, Mr K. Parrott, Mr Christopher Pick, Miss Jean Rendell, Professor R. Spence, Mr A. A. Tait, Dr Geoffrey Templeman and Mr H. C. Thomas.

Finally, I am most grateful for the help and advice of Mr Stanley Meyrick, Chief Architect to the UGC, who has taken such an active interest in this book.

Bibliography

References shown by superior numbers in the text are indicated in brackets after the title of the work.

Beloff, Michael. *The Plateglass Universities* (18). London 1968
Brawne, Michael (ed.). *University Planning and Design* (5, 13). London 1967
Caine, Sir Sydney. *British Universities: Purpose and Prospects* (2). London 1969
Clossick, Marie. *Student Residence*. London 1967
Daiches, D. (ed.). *The Idea of a New University: an Experiment in Sussex*. London 1964
Dober, Richard P. *Campus Planning*. New York 1964
Gombrich, E. H. *Art and Illusion* (15). London 1960
Mathew, Johnson-Marshall. *Development Plan 1962–72* (9). York 1962
Metcalf, Keyes D. *Planning Academic and Research Libraries*. New York 1965
Neal, K. W. *British University Libraries*. Manchester 1970
Perkin, H. J. *New Universities in the United Kingdom*. Paris 1969
Robbins, Lord. *Committee on Higher Education: Report*. London 1963
Sloman, Albert E. *A University in the Making* (16). London 1964
Thompson, E. P. (ed.). *Warwick University Ltd* (17). London 1970
University Grants Committee. *Annual Survey 1969–70* (1). London 1971

> *Report of the Committee on Libraries* (Parry). London 1967
> *Report of the Sub-committee on Halls of Residence* (3). London 1957
> *Student Residence (Planning and Construction of Halls of Residence)*. London 1967
> *University Development 1962–67*. London 1968
> *University Development: Notes on Procedure 1969*. London 1970

Among the numerous architectural and other periodicals publishing articles on university design and progress, the following are of particular interest.
Architect and Building News, 8 May 1968. *Architects' Journal*, 6 November 1963, 14 December 1966, 21 December 1966, 21 February 1968, 6 March 1968 (4). *Architectural Review, The*, October 1963, July 1964, April 1970 (New Universities issue) (7). *Country Life*, 3 October 1963 (8). *FUSS* (Forum for University Staff and Students, University of Kent at Canterbury), February 1971 (14). *RIBA Journal*, April 1965 (10, 11, 12). *Royal Society of Arts Journal*, July 1965 (6). *Sunday Times Magazine*, 12 October–30 November 1969.